CHICAGO
CABLE CARS

GREG BORZO

Charleston · London

THE
History
PRESS

This scene at State and Madison Streets looking northeast in 1904 includes not only cable cars but also horse-drawn vehicles, an electric trolley car being towed at the back of a cable train and the latest transportation newcomer, an automobile. The State Street cable train on the left is heading south to 63rd Street, and the one on the right is heading east onto one of six downtown cable car loops. *Chicago Transit Authority.*

Published by The History Press
Charleston, SC 29403
www.historypress.net

Front cover: A Chicago City Railway cable car train on the South Side, circa 1900. *Crerar Library, University of Chicago*. Unless otherwise noted, images are from the author's collection.

First published 2012

Manufactured in the United States

ISBN 978.1.60949.327.1

Library of Congress CIP data applied for.

I dedicate this book to my fellow book club members who over many years have motivated me to read more, suggested fascinating books and shared their thoughts and feelings concerning many topics.

Almost three decades ago, Christine Bertrand, Gina Ferrera and Martha Barry formed our first book club. I thought the idea was too ambitious because people did not read much anymore. I was wrong, as demonstrated by the long parade of voracious readers who enthusiastically joined our ranks. Reading is and always will be interesting and inspiring, as well as vital to the health of society. Thank you, fellow readers, for reminding me of this, month after month.

A list of all the readers who have participated in our various book clubs over the years would be too long. Here are my current fellow book club members, to whom I am deeply grateful for their fun companionship and stimulating conversation:

Martha Barry, Christine Bertrand, Mary Blumer Reed, Sherry Brenner, Mary Bryant, Emily Clout, Maury Collins, Steve Doroba, Gina Ferrera, Dave Ihnat, Chris James, Kathy Kennedy, Terry Kennedy, Mike Nolan, Doug Nystrom, Nancy Oda, Kateri O'Shea, Jim Pryma, Renee Ribant, Jack Scanlon, Christine Slivon, Dennis Smerko, Marcia Smith, Mike Smyth, Tina Stretch, Jane Swanson-Nystrom and Kevan Wifvat. You are the best!

CONTENTS

NOT TO BE FORGOTTEN

Ask most Chicagoans what comes to mind when you mention "cable cars" and they'll no doubt mention "San Francisco." This comes as no surprise, as that city's image is forever intertwined with the cable car. However, most Chicagoans would be surprised to learn that their own city once had cable cars—even one of the largest cable car systems in the world. In fact, many have walked by, driven past or even dined in remnants of Chicago's cable car heritage without realizing it.

Such is often the case with Chicago history. It's hidden in plain sight. While Chicago is known as a city that sheds its skin every few decades, tearing down the old to build anew, there are more remnants of the old around than many people recognize. When one delves deeper, these remnants tell oft-overlooked stories of integral chapters in Chicago's history.

Cable cars are an important chapter. While Chicago's history often gets told in reference to its ideal location, the national transportation networks it cultivated and the massive population boom it experienced due to these conditions, local transportation often gets little mention or study. But Chicago never would have become such a boomtown if local residents could not have gotten to the factory gate, office tower or department store. It took the planning and development of local transportation networks for that to happen.

The story of the cable car in Chicago fits in at a key time in the city's growth. In the 1880s, the city was in the process of becoming an industrial powerhouse. The first electric trolley and the "L" line were still a few years off. Rickety and unsanitary horsecars were not going to cut it; the city needed a modern, innovative solution to the challenge of local transportation. San Francisco provided the model for cable cars, but Chicago's system quickly overtook that city's system in both ridership and equipment.

Cable cars were essential to everyday life in Chicago. A North Chicago Street Railroad cable train heads south on Lincoln Avenue just past Wrightwood Avenue after the Schiller Theater opened in 1892 but before the theater changed its name to the Garrick in 1903. Cable cars carried more than one *billion* riders during their quarter-century run in Chicago. *Chicago History Museum.*

The success of Chicago's cable cars played a large role in tying together outlying areas of the city in the early stages of its growth. Transit-oriented development may be a present-day urban planning concept, but it aptly describes what happened when the cable car lines were built. Outlying areas grew, and new housing, retail and industrial developments were constructed at a brisk pace, at least in parts of Chicago. The relatively faster speeds of the cable cars allowed residents to live farther from the center of the city and to commute downtown for work each day. And while Chicago neighborhoods may have a reputation for being parochial enclaves, they were knitted together by extensive transit lines, including those provided by cable cars, in networks that helped them relate to the city as a whole and participate in its economy.

While they may be forgotten now, cable cars were an essential part of life in Chicago for one-quarter of a century. They provided reliable transportation for city residents, reliable wages for their employees and reliable profits for their owners and investors. Studying the tenure of the cable car in Chicago provides a fascinating window into everyday life, the business environment, urban growth and transit history during an important period of the city's history.

Like most inventions, the cable car was doomed to eventual obsolescence. The electric trolley replaced it as a more efficient, comfortable and profitable form of transportation. Just as some of the first skyscrapers were being torn down and replaced with "new and improved structures," the cable car system was scrapped and became just a memory. Later, not even that.

Although cable cars departed the Chicago scene more than a century ago, there are still physical remnants of the cable car system present in the city today. As you learn about the history of the system in the pages ahead, you will discover that there are some obvious and prominent structures remaining from that system. These structures provide a physical link to the system's history, as well as to the history of Chicago's development. One can stand in front of them and imagine what it would have been like to stand in the same place more than one hundred years earlier, listening to the whir of steam engines, the hum of underground cables and the clang of cable car gongs. Such tangible connections to our past are vital and should be recognized and cherished.

While it might be easy to cast a long-gone urban cable car system as an obscure bit of history, this attitude neglects the vital, albeit brief, role cable cars played in Chicago. Local transportation improvements were essential to Chicago's competitiveness as an increasingly important industrial city. Cable cars served dense, transit-oriented streets that were later served by electric trolleys and still exist today, streets such as Cottage Grove Avenue, Clark Street, Milwaukee Avenue and numerous others.

So as you read and look at the photographs in the coming pages, keep in mind how much influence cable cars had on the growth of Chicago. When you are walking, biking, driving or using public transportation to get around the city, think about the cable cars and how central they were to Chicago's advancement into a great metropolis. While they existed for only about one-quarter of a century, cable cars had a profound influence on Chicago that is still visible and relevant today.

Jacob Kaplan
Editor and Co-founder of Forgotten Chicago
www.forgottenchicago.com

ACKNOWLEDGEMENTS

This book would never have come together without tremendous help from many people and organizations. First and foremost is Roy G. Benedict of Publishers' Services, whose encouragement, guidance and knowledge lit the way. Roy is a leading authority on Chicago's cable cars. He is also an expert mapmaker, and his meticulous maps inform this text. Roy is also a talented editor. In addition, he maintains a library of records, documents, books, photographs and even unpublished typescripts about Chicago's street railways that he openly shared with me. His patience and generosity set a high standard that everyone should emulate.

Gathering photographs of Chicago's cable cars—a distant, forgotten topic—was not easy. The Chicago Transit Authority (CTA) was extremely helpful in this regard. Special thanks go to Joyce Shaw for coordinating this effort. Michael Williams generously provided enhanced versions of several of the CTA's photographs.

Many others provided photographs, leads on other photographs and help interpreting these images. For this I am indebted to Roy Benedict; David Clark; Michael Dorf; George Kanary; Julie Lynch at the Sulzer Regional Library's Northside Neighborhood History Collection; Lesley Martin at the Chicago History Museum's Research Center; Dennis McClendon at Chicago CartoGraphics; Stephen L. Meyers; Bruce Moffat; Gary Niederkorn at the International Brotherhood of Electrical Workers; Nick Ohlman at the Museum of Transportation in St. Louis; Art Peterson; and Morag Walsh at the Harold Washington Library Center's Special Collections and Preservation Division.

Jonathan Michael Johnson shot striking, contemporary photographs of cable car remnants all over Chicago. Owner and founder of Planck Studios (www.planckstudios.com), Jonathan is an extremely talented, award-winning photographer.

ACKNOWLEDGEMENTS

The following libraries and organizations provided invaluable research opportunities and assistance: Chicago Public Library, Chicago History Museum, University of Chicago's Crerar Library, Hyde Park Historical Society, Newberry Library and Northwestern University's Transportation Library. Jenna Nigro in Special Collections at the Daley Library at the University of Illinois at Chicago was especially helpful.

Jill Donovan and Rob Bagstad of JDRB Design provided excellent graphics.

Hard copies of books, maps and reports will always be important, but Google Books played a surprisingly large role in my research. An incredible and growing number of sources are available through this free online service. Better yet, these sources are searchable and easily available 24/7 from any Internet-enabled computer.

No book is complete without thorough, painstaking proofreading. Sherry Brenner and John Greenfield attacked this job with care and enthusiasm. They did a wonderful job improving the text.

INTRODUCTION

CHICAGO'S CENTRAL ROLE IN CABLE CAR HISTORY

In the 1880s, people around the world looked to Chicago, then the fastest-growing city, to see what the future would hold in terms of urban life, public works, finance, commerce—and transit. On January 28, 1882, they would have seen cable cars beginning to operate on State Street.

On that cold, blustery day, Chicagoans packed both sides of State Street from Madison Street to the new cable car powerhouse at 21st Street. Crowds estimated from 50,000 to an improbable 300,000 waited hours with great anticipation to witness the first cable car trains pass by. Chicago City Railway (CCR) had promised something revolutionary: street railway cars pulled by a clean, quiet, *invisible* force with the capacity to carry an unheralded hundreds of passengers per train.

The crowd was apprehensive about the risk their city had undertaken. Property owners claimed cable lines would ruin their businesses. Horsecar companies worried the new technology would put them out of work. Horse owners asserted the cable cars would frighten their steeds. Residents feared the horseless streetcars traveling up to eight miles per hour would maim or kill them.

But there was no holding back. This was a city that had raised itself from muddy swamps, made itself the nation's railroad hub, built the Union Stock Yards, recovered from a devastating fire and was in the process of reversing a river and inventing the skyscraper. Cable cars would be another sensational achievement. CCR was about to demonstrate that the cable car was the best transit solution available anywhere in the world.

At 2:30 p.m., the first cable car train carried the Lyon and Healy band. The second one included eight cars filled with CCR officials, civic leaders and assorted dignitaries. Both trains seemed to glide along effortlessly, driven by the "concealed power" of an underground cable—a completely new form of motive power for Chicago transit.

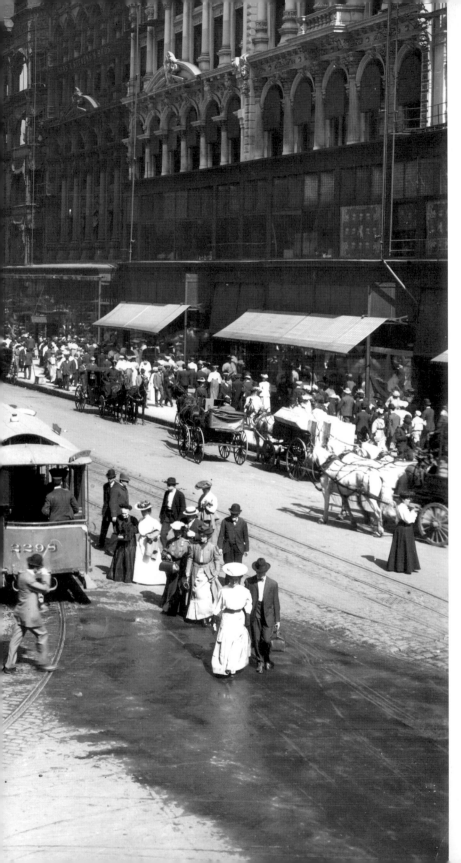

A nationwide cable car boom started on State Street in 1882. Here, a Madison Street cable train turns north at State Street between 1902 and 1906 on one of West Chicago Street Railroad's downtown cable car loops. To avoid crossing other cable tracks, cable trains on State Street north of Madison Street operated on the left side of the street, against the flow of traffic.

The jubilant crowds gathered along State Street were not disappointed. "In spite of the general prediction that they would jump off the tracks, it was agreed universally that they were the airiest and most graceful vehicles of the sort ever seen in Chicago or anywhere else," reported the *Chicago Tribune*.

With civic pride, one rider described the cable line as "the most gigantic undertaking ever attempted by any street railway company…It marked an era of wonderful improvement in the construction and operation of street railways in Chicago."

Thus, it was in the burgeoning city of Chicago—not in San Francisco—"where in the midst of frost and snow, and on *level* roads embracing curves of peculiar difficulty, that the [cable car] system was triumphantly demonstrated to be of general applicability," wrote James Clifton Robinson, general manager of the Los Angeles Cable Railway, in 1891.

Almost twenty-five years later, however, Chicago bid an "unregretful," even unkind, farewell to its degraded, increasingly derided cable cars. By then, the electric trolley had eclipsed the cable car, which had become a millstone for the city.

As each cable line closed forever, rowdies stormed trains, overturning cars and stripping them of souvenirs. The *San Francisco Call* reported that on July 22, 1906, the last cable cars on State Street made a pathetic exit: "Groaning and wobbling as one decrepit and having earned a long rest, the final cable train [on that line] rattled and bumped around the loop and swung into position for its 'positively last performance' at 1:35 o'clock a.m. The train consisted of a battered grip car and a twenty-year-old trailer…By the time the old cars reached their destination they were much splintered and smashed by 'relic hunters.'" Then, on August 19, a mob destroyed the penultimate Madison Street cable train. The next and last train on that line required police protection to proceed. And on October 21, Chicago's *very* last cable train met its inglorious end traveling south from downtown on the Cottage Grove Avenue line to the 39th Street car barn. When the engines were turned off at the 21st Street powerhouse, Chicago's cable car era ended at the same location where it had begun in 1882.

⁝

How and why Chicago embraced the cable car with the abandon of a young lover only to reject it as a dinosaur a scant quarter of a century later is a fascinating yet virtually unknown story. The story has been overlooked for so long that it runs the risk of being completely forgotten. Countless Chicago history books skip over cable cars, passing from horsecars directly to electric trolley cars. Meanwhile, many of the books that do refer to cable cars confuse them with trolleys.

This rare, hand-tinted photo shows Chicago City Railway cable trains passing on Wabash Avenue in front of the Auditorium Building after the building was completed in 1889 but before the Loop "L" was completed one block north in 1897. The Cottage Grove train in the center is heading south to 39th Street. *Courtesy of Bruce Moffat.*

Vital to the city's growth and development for slightly less than twenty-five years, cable cars helped Chicago's economy prosper by employing thousands of people and carrying an enormous number of riders to work, shopping and entertainment venues. More than one *billion* cable car fares were collected in Chicago. Cable cars helped Chicago expand, especially on the South Side, where cable line extensions south of 39th Street increased the city's reach into areas that were relatively unsettled.

In addition, this is a story with a national scope. During its cable car era, Chicago had more cable car passengers than any other city. Cable car ridership numbers are hard to come by, but ridership peaked nationwide at about 400 million passengers in 1894, and more than 80 million of them were in Chicago.

Chicago also had more cable cars than any other city, perhaps as many as three thousand. And with a peak of 41.2 double-track route miles (82.4 single-track miles), Chicago had more cable car miles than any other city except San Francisco, which peaked at 52.8 double-track miles.

Thirteen powerhouses in Chicago pulled thirty-four separate cables adding up to some 500,000 feet in length and weighing 750 tons. The total investment in Chicago's cable cars and infrastructure exceeded $25 million (about $600 million in today's dollars, using 1890 as the base year). Furthermore, this book will show that Chicago played *the* central role in the growth and development of cable cars throughout the country.

☙❧

The beginning and the end of the cable car story illustrate survival of the fittest. The cable car flourished for a short period between the horsecar and the electric trolley car. It improved upon the horsecar because a cable line was much cheaper to operate per mile than a horsecar line (eleven cents per car mile versus twenty-two cents per car mile, respectively, in Chicago in 1898).

Soon thereafter, however, the trolley car trumped the cable car—based not on operating costs, which were similar, but on the fact that it was much cheaper to build a trolley line than a cable line (about 10 percent of the $100,000 to $300,000 per mile it cost to build a cable line). Once the electric trolley demonstrated its potential in Montgomery, Alabama, in 1886, the end of the cable car era was inevitable. By 1890, electric trolley mileage was double that of cable car mileage, and the cable car was doomed.

If the inventors and entrepreneurs behind the cable car had perfected their system as early as the 1840s—when all the essential pieces of the technology were available—the cable car would have had a much longer run in Chicago and nationwide. On the other hand, if those inventors and entrepreneurs had been just five or six years slower than they were, not a single mile of cable car track would ever have been built in Chicago.

Opposite: Cable cars operated in Chicago for almost twenty-five years from 1882 to 1906—well beyond 1895, when mileage began to drop nationwide. It did not drop in Chicago until 1906 but then did so precipitously. *JDRB Design, Chicago.*

Miles of U.S. Cable Car Lines
1873–1910

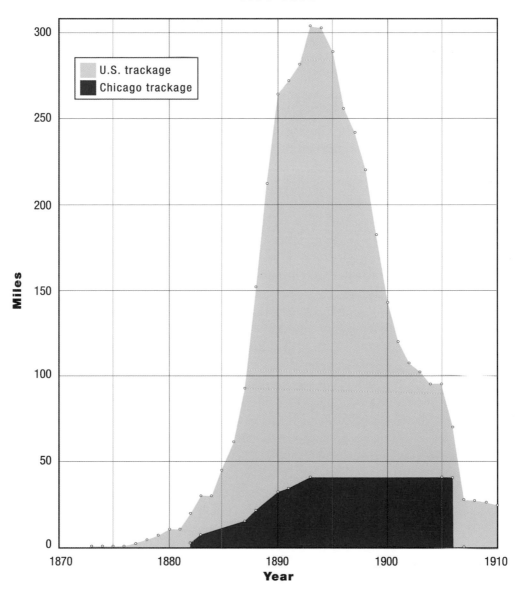

Peak double track miles per year. Single track with traffic in both directions is counted as double track. Single track with traffic in one direction is counted as half of double track.

Source: *The Cable Car in America* by George Hilton

ഔCഔR

Cable cars were central not only to Chicago's growth and urban morphology but also to the nation's transit history and urban development.

With few exceptions, early Americans did not ride horses around their settlements. They walked. As villages grew into towns during the second half of the nineteenth century in the rapidly urbanizing United States, residents found it impracticable or increasingly difficult to walk everywhere they wanted to go. Little by little, tinkerers and inventors devised public conveyances to carry residents from one destination to another. In fits and starts, entrepreneurs and businessmen, engineers and builders, city officials and transit companies realized some of these dreams and schemes. They built various local, fixed-route, fare-based, open-to-the-public urban transportation systems—what we now call transit.

Eventually, transit evolved into a huge and enormously important industry nationwide. From the 1870s to the 1910s, transit represented the veritable circulatory system of every U.S. city. In 1881, on the eve of Chicago's first cable car line, there were 415 street railways operating eighteen thousand cars over three thousand miles of track in the United States. They employed thirty-five thousand people and collected an astonishing $1.2 billion in fares. Most of these passengers traveled in horsecars— but once Chicago ignited the nationwide interest in cable car technology in 1882, passengers increasingly rode cable cars.

That year, the American Street Railway Association was created to represent the burgeoning transit industry. The representative from Chicago City Railway could not attend the association's first meeting in Boston because he was too busy working on a new cable car line in Chicago. But in one of the first orders of business at that meeting, delegates selected Chicago as the site for their second annual meeting. They were eager to inspect the new cable car installation there.

ഔCഔR

Transit cars not only carried people to their desired destinations; they also brought people together—physically and even socially—in a public space, similar to the way a plaza or park brings people together, where different kinds of people gather together and experience or even engage each other. Being much larger and more popular than horsecars, cable cars enlarged and expanded upon this shared public space that transit creates. Thus, riding in a cable car had a humanizing and democratizing effect on the populace. Everyone could and almost everyone did ride; when they did, they became more aware of and familiar with their fellow city dwellers. For many Chicagoans, taking the cable car became a rich part of the very fabric of everyday life.

As the newest and best form of transit in the 1880s, cable cars reflected the pride of their builders, the companies that operated them and the cities where they operated. Their varnished wood, polished fittings, vivid color schemes, ornate interiors and decorated exteriors made the cars elegant symbols of a new urban way of life. They were not only a utilitarian way to get around; in addition, they were eye-catching and popular. Chicagoans in the early 1880s were proud that their city was one of the first to offer cable cars—this slick, ballyhooed form of transit. They flocked to the cars and clamored for more lines. Many Chicagoans rode cable cars simply for fun and excitement.

"Every man, woman, and child in Chicago now points to the cable cars as one of the most valuable and progressive enterprises of Chicago," said the *Inter Ocean* in August 1885. "The citizen enjoys a quiet chuckle as he does homage to his own superior knowledge at the expense of the mystified looks and questions of his country cousin."

A WCSR cable train heads east on Madison Street, as seen from the "L" platform on 5th Avenue (now Wells Street). The track on the left has no slot because it was used only by horsecars. The *Record* was a local newspaper. *Library of Congress.*

ഇരുജ

What was Chicago like in 1882, when men sported handlebar mustaches, women endured corsets and everyone wore a hat?

Over the previous ten years, Chicago's population had doubled to 600,000. The city was well on its way to recovering from the Great Fire of 1871. Up-and-coming railroads tore through town, their tracks crisscrossing the city.

The Chicago River and its branches divided the city into three "divisions"—North, West and South—each one somewhat isolated from the others due to the limited number of bridges and the frequent openings of these moveable bridges to allow numerous cargo boats to pass. Incredibly vibrant and crowded with pedestrians and vehicles, the downtown had nowhere to go but up. This crowding was beginning to give rise to impressive, tall buildings. The ten-story Montauk Building, constructed in 1882, was the country's first building to be labeled a "skyscraper. "

Also in 1882, Charles Tyson Yerkes had just moved to Chicago. Having made a fortune in Philadelphia as a financier, he set out to make another fortune in Chicago through transit. Finding ways to profit at every level—planning, financing, building, operating, buying and selling transit lines—Yerkes became known as the "Chicago Cable Car Czar" because he was responsible for building and operating cable lines in two of the city's three divisions. Having established Chicago as the world's leading cable car city, the "Transit Titan" and "Goliath of Graft" is central to our story. *Scientific American* said in 1893 that Yerkes "combined the successful elements of a general, financier, politician…abilities which in most other avenues of trade would suffice for four men."

೫⊃⊂೪

Many historians have exaggerated San Francisco's early role and shunned Chicago's vital role in the nation's cable car era. Prior to Chicago's first installation, the cable car was regarded as a novel solution to climbing steep hills in San Francisco, a small, distant West Coast city in a country dominated by the East Coast. At the time of Chicago's first installation, San Francisco had only five relatively short, straight cable lines totaling 11.2 double-track miles.

It was CCR that brought the cable car technology to prominence by proving that the cable car could serve a large, flat city with cold winters. As a result, the technology spread around the country. Ultimately, sixty-five companies built cable lines in twenty-nine U.S. cities, peaking at 305 double-track miles. They invested $125 million in the necessary infrastructure (about $3 billion in today's dollars, using 1890 as the base

Opposite: An unusually long four-car Clark Street cable train heads west on Randolph Street approaching LaSalle Street. The old Cook County Court House and City Hall on the right was replaced with the current Chicago City Hall and County Building beginning in 1906, the same year Chicago's cable cars bit the dust. The Masonic Temple, at twenty-two stories once the city's tallest building, is in the background. *Library of Congress.*

year). After CCR opened its first line in 1882, the *Chicago Tribune* predicted, "It may reasonably be expected that this cable-line on State Street will revolutionize the street-car system not only in Chicago but in every large city in the country."

If CCR had not built its cable line in 1882, the cable car might well have been confined to San Francisco. The next hilly city to build cable lines was Kansas City, but not until 1890, by which time electric trolley technology was advanced enough to tackle some of that city's hills. If not for CCR's daring installation in 1882, horses would have continued as the main source of transit traction in Chicago and everywhere else around the country until the electric trolley car technology was mastered in 1886.

Therefore, January 28, 1882, when CCR began operating Chicago's first cable line on State Street, was the most important date in the history of the cable car. The events of that day in Chicago propelled the technology into the limelight and initiated a nationwide cable car building boom.

"While San Francisco was the pioneer in the adoption of the cable system, impelled thereto by the steep grades of its streets, Chicago has proved the adaptability of the plan in a northern climate and for a level surface, and the successful demonstration of the principle here has been the means of introducing it in many other cities," said *Railway Age* from the perspective of 1886. "The cable now seems destined to take the place of horses for street car movement in cities quite generally."

CHAPTER 1

HOW CABLE CARS WORK

In 1889, the celebrated poet and novelist Rudyard Kipling visited San Francisco. Like others encountering cable cars for the first time, he found them mysterious, even magical. In a letter to a friend he wrote:

> Cable-cars have for all practical purposes made San Francisco dead level. They take no count of rise or fall, but slide equably on their appointed courses…They turn corners almost at right angles; cross other lines and, for aught I know, may run up the sides of houses. There is no visible agency of their flight, but once in a while you pass a five-storied building humming with machinery that winds up an everlasting wire-cable, and the initiated will tell you that here is the mechanism. I gave up asking questions. If it pleases Providence to make a car run up and down a slit in the ground for many miles, and if for two pence and halfpenny I can ride in that car, why should I seek the reasons of the miracle?

Contrary to Kipling's stance, we shall seek the "reasons of the miracle." And we shall see that the "miracle" is merely mechanical. At its simplest level, cable car operation depends on four components: the continuously moving cable; the grip underneath each grip car that grabs or releases the cable; the underground conduit through which the cable circulates; and the powerhouse that keeps the cable moving.

Although designing and building Chicago's cable car system demanded technical knowhow and a mastery of mechanical minutiae, the basic concept behind cable car operation is straightforward: cars move forward by gripping the continuously moving underground cable and stop by releasing the cable and applying brakes.

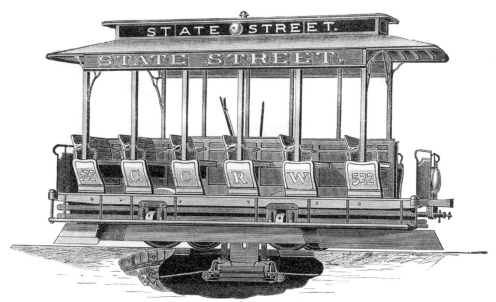

Grip Car, Showing Cable in Grip as When Drawing a Train.

A grip car holds the cable in its grip to move forward. In release mode, the cable would drop from the grip onto carrying pulleys below. The warning gong is near the top of the roof between "State" and "Street." *Courtesy of David Clark.*

THE CABLE

At the heart of Chicago's cable car system was a thick, super-strong wire cable. The most common type of cable consisted of a hemp rope core around which six steel wires were wound. Each of these six wires consisted of sixteen smaller wire strands that were, themselves, wound together. Thus, the cable included ninety-six individual wire strands bundled together around a rope core.

A rope core made the cable more flexible than if the cable had been made entirely of steel wires. This flexibility reduced wear, made curves and turns easier to handle and reduced rigidity when a load was applied, thereby diminishing the chance of breakage.

The diameter of the cable ranged from $7/8$ to $1\frac{1}{2}$ inches, but $1\frac{1}{8}$ to $1\frac{1}{4}$ inches was most common. Cable weighed about three pounds per foot or eight tons per mile. Chicago's longest single cable was on Chicago City Railway's (CCR) Cottage

Grove Avenue line and measured 27,770 feet, or 5.3 miles. The longest single cable anywhere was 43,700 feet—an astonishing 8.3 miles—on Lexington Avenue in New York, but this route had minimal curves and only one short grade.

Most cable car lines in Chicago incorporated several individual cables with trains passing from one cable to the next along the way. For example, the Milwaukee Avenue line incorporated three cables. As it left the car barn at Armitage Avenue, a cable car grabbed onto a 20,500-foot cable. As it passed the powerhouse at Cleaver Street heading southeast on Milwaukee Avenue, the car let go of the first cable and picked up a 20,100-foot one. Both of these cables were driven from the Cleaver Street powerhouse. At Jefferson and Washington Streets, the car let go of the second cable and picked up a 10,200-foot one that was driven by the powerhouse at that intersection. This third cable pulled the car through the Washington Street tunnel and around a single-track downtown loop. The return trip reversed the sequence of cables.

It may seem that the cable was a simple matter—certainly less complicated than the grip, conduit or machinery that kept the cable moving. Nevertheless, it was not a standard item routinely ordered off the shelf. Selecting the best cable for the layout and configuration of each section of each line was an art that demanded attention to detail and required trade-offs. For example, a thick cable lasted longer but was more expensive, heavier to move and harder to handle. A high-tensile cable was stronger than regular steel but somewhat brittle, especially in the cold, where it tended to break on curves. And the so-called Lang lay cable wore out smoothly (rather than becoming fragmented with broken strands) but was difficult to splice.

As specialists considered such trade-offs, they tried to match the best cable—which varied in diameter, weight, quality of fabrication, type of steel, cost, number of strands and direction of winding—to each particular application. And each application varied in length, grade, number and type of curves, operating speed, average and peak ridership, type of grip used, time of year and weather.

Maintaining the wire and coaxing the most possible miles out of it was a demanding science that required not only vigilance but also specialized knowledge. Typically, one cable would provide 40,000 to 150,000 miles of service over about eight months before wearing out. It was not uncommon, however, for a cable to last more than one year only to have its replacement last three or four months due to different operating conditions, weather and other factors. CCR averaged 280 days from two straight cables that ran south of 39th Street; 114 days from cables that ran over two curves south of 21st Street; but only 90 days from its downtown loop cables.

Temperature, age, load, operating practices and other factors changed the cable's dimensions. Typically, a new cable stretched 1 to 2 percent, especially in the first few weeks of service. During its lifetime of stretching and wear, a cable could add more than two hundred feet in length and lose about $^3/_{16}$ of an inch in diameter.

In the late 1880s, a twenty-five-thousand-foot cable cost about $6,000 to $7,000, including shipping. Given such costs, maintenance was a priority, and the condition of each cable was monitored closely. Workers impregnated the internal hemp core with hot tar that remained in a semi-liquid form during operation, providing lubrication and waterproofing. They oiled the exterior of the cable to prevent whatever tar seeped

A wagon built in the 1880s to haul cables in St. Louis and Cincinnati illustrates the cable's great weight. It carried sixty tons, "the biggest load ever hauled on two axles and four wheels," the company claimed. *Museum of Transportation.*

out from gumming up the grip, winding equipment or carrying rollers. They reapplied this coating regularly, sometimes daily, because rain or a flood could wash off the oil and allow the cable to corrode.

Every night, the cable was shut down for inspection and maintenance. Inspectors could predict fairly accurately when a cable needed to be replaced by keeping a sharp eye on the number and size of loose strands, as well as the diameter of a cable. Due to a reel's immense size and weight and the long distances such reels typically traveled from a manufacturer, it could take weeks to get a replacement cable. Therefore, Chicago's cable car companies kept huge reels of various types and lengths of cable on hand for replacements—planned or otherwise.

Delivering a reel of cable from a railroad siding to a cable car powerhouse was challenging and required enormous wagons pulled by dozens, even scores of horses. Once delivered, the replacement cable was spliced onto the old cable and run through the system. The old cable was recycled as scrap.

If a cable broke unexpectedly in service, a temporary splice could be made in the field. A permanent splice would be made that night in the powerhouse while the system was shut down. Splicing was a highly valued specialty craft. The splicer worked his trade with a vise, wire cutters, tongs, mallets and chisels. The splice had to have exactly the same diameter as the cable; otherwise, it could catch on the grip and kink the cable. Splices ran about sixty feet long, and a good one was as strong as the original cable.

THE GRIP

The grip could be likened to a three-hundred-pound pair of pliers. Operated by the gripman with a large lever, it held the grip car to the cable in a vise-like hold. There were top, bottom and side grips, as well as single-jaw and double-jaw grips, but they all operated on the same principle. Chicago's three cable car companies used four noncompatible grips.

The gripping mechanism was much too large to fit through the narrow slot in the middle of the track. Therefore, it was fastened to the bottom of a thin metal shank that was narrow enough to fit through the slot. At the start of each day, the grip had to be lowered into the underground conduit through a trap, a large opening in the slot or a large opening in the track.

When the gripman pulled his lever all the way back to "full grip," the jaws of the grip tightened around the cable. In "partial release," the loosely held cable passed

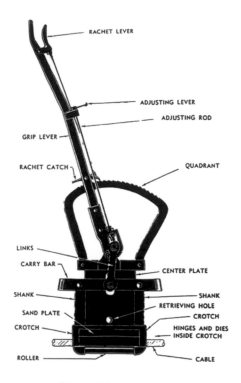

RACHET LEVER

ADJUSTING LEVER

ADJUSTING ROD

GRIP LEVER

RACHET CATCH

QUADRANT

LINKS

CARRY BAR

CENTER PLATE

SHANK

SHANK

SAND PLATE

RETRIEVING HOLE

CROTCH

CROTCH

HINGES AND DIES
INSIDE CROTCH

ROLLER

CABLE

GRIP DIAGRAM

Components of a bottom grip. Pulling the lever backward lowered the grip and tightened it around the cable. Pushing the lever forward released the cable and raised the grip.

through the grip. In "full release," the open grip allowed the cable to drop entirely out of its jaws onto carrying rollers in the conduit. The exact points for each lever to partially release or fully release the cable were not set; rather, they varied by type of grip as well as the individual grip itself. Through training and experience, a seasoned gripman knew how to feel the cable in his grip.

The gripman would drop the cable at let-go points. These occurred upon transition to the next cable along a route; at curves where trains coasted around a corner; at intersections with another cable line; and at the end of the trip or day. After coasting through the dead spot, the gripman had to pick up the cable again, often with the help of specially placed guiding pulleys buried in the conduit. These pulleys raised the cable to the height of the grip and moved it into the grip's jaws. Failing that, the conductor could use a greased hook to fish around in the conduit and lift the cable into the grip.

Semi-cylindrical pads (called "dies" at the time) inside the jaw of the grip were the only part of the grip that came into contact with the cable. Made of soft steel to achieve a good tactile hold, the twelve- to eighteen-inch-long pads wore out quickly and needed to be replaced every five to ten days, depending on the traffic and load. To compensate for the gradual wear on the pads, thicker jaw linings were used or the jaw was progressively tightened.

It is amazing that the relatively small grip mechanism could transfer enough of the cable's power to haul a grip car and several trailers, each of which could be loaded with up to ninety people. The grip took a toll on the cable every time it grabbed the cable and whenever the cable slid through the grip in partial release. One engineer estimated that contact with the grip was responsible for three-fourths of the wear and tear on the cable. Contact with rollers, pulleys and sheaves (grooved wheels) in the conduit was responsible for the rest.

Four different types of grips were used in Chicago; they were not compatible. Dozens of additional designs were used around the country. A pilot wheel controlled this unusual one on the Missouri Railroad in St. Louis. *Museum of Transportation.*

THE CONDUIT

The most expensive component of a cable car system was the conduit that ran directly underneath the track. Through this channel twenty to forty inches below ground, the cable circulated continuously on carrying rollers (called "pulleys" at the time) located every thirty to forty feet. These rollers were nine to twenty-four inches in diameter, depending on the preference of the engineer, as well as the clearance and design of the line. Together with strategically placed bars and sheaves, these rollers kept the cable on its appointed rounds.

The first cable car conduits constructed in San Francisco in 1873 were made of iron bars, ties and planks fastened together, but the parts loosened, warped and fell out of line. In 1878, the California Street Cable Railroad improved upon this flimsy design, using iron yokes set in concrete, which quickly became standard.

Each yoke weighed three to four hundred pounds and was about five feet wide, four feet deep and six to eight inches thick. These colossi had to be laid in the ground with great precision at approximately five-foot intervals. At the same time, the rollers and sheaves had to be aligned meticulously. The whole operation required "the utmost nicety of construction and finish," as one builder put it.

Although a well-built, water- and weather-resistant conduit was essential for cable cars to spread beyond San Francisco, its high cost discouraged installation of new cable systems. At about $60,000 to $150,000 per mile to build, the conduit accounted for approximately 60 percent of the cost of building a cable system.

Conduits were overbuilt to provide stability for the slot, minimize variations in the width of the slot and prevent the slot from caving in under the weight of heavy road vehicles, such as fire wagons. Conduits were so strong that the weight of cable cars and passengers on the rails was relatively inconsequential.

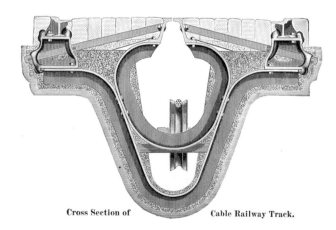

Cross Section of   **Cable Railway Track.**

Cross section of cable car conduit and track structure. Note the cross section of the cable riding on a carrying roller and the narrow slot through which the grip's shank would pass. *Courtesy of David Clark.*

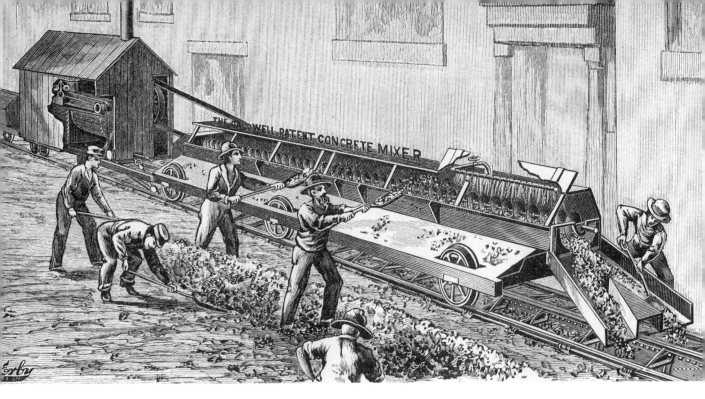

A steam-driven concrete mixer that NCSR used to pour concrete around yokes and cable car track structure. *Chicago History Museum.*

The conduit's heavy-duty design was critical to keeping the slot open. Ideally, the slot was a constant ¾ inch wide to accommodate the grip's ½-inch-wide metal shank with minimal friction (plus a small amount of clearance). A narrower slot would have restricted movement of the shank. A wider slot would have allowed excess dirt and debris to collect on the bottom of the conduit. Also, a wider slot ran the risk of snagging the calk of a horseshoe or trapping a carriage wheel, some of which were as thin as ⅞ inch wide.

In cold weather, the water that surrounded and seeped into a conduit's foundation could freeze and expand. In the summer, the yokes and other metal parts could expand due to the heat. In either case, the expansion would squeeze the slot to the point that the movement of the shank could be impeded or even blocked.

Building Chicago's conduits involved digging a trench about three feet wide and four feet deep with side bays every five feet to accommodate the wide yokes. To create a solid, level foundation, crews filled in depressions and drove piles into swamps. Workers had to relocate gas mains, water pipes, sewer lines and other obstacles they encountered under streets. Engineers had to assure drainage for the conduit. This was accomplished by connecting to the city's sewers or building a new drainage system, the latter of which added considerably to the cost.

Pulleys and sheaves at termini, curves and inclines kept the cable in its optimal position, vertically and horizontally. At each turnaround point, the cable reversed direction on a ten- to twelve-foot-diameter sheave mounted horizontally in a reinforced brick or concrete underground vault so that it could carry cable cars back in the other direction.

Ideally, cable routes were built in a straight line, but curves were needed in Chicago, despite its grid-like layout. Difficult to engineer and build and troublesome to operate, curves were known as the bane of cable cars. "Their first cost is enormous; they consume power; materially shorten the life of the [cable]; and are a source of endless care and anxiety to management," said C.B. Fairchild, editor of *Street Railway Journal*, in 1892.

There were two ways for cable cars to negotiate a curve. With the let-go curve, the gripman let go of the cable, thereby allowing the train to coast around the curve through

A six-foot-diameter sheave dug up in the late 1930s or early 1940s from a cable car vault under State Street between Madison and Monroe Streets. Sheaves, rollers and pulleys guided the cable along its underground path. *Chicago Transit Authority.*

momentum. After the train negotiated the curve, the gripman picked up the cable again. Relatively simple to build, let-go curves were limited to locations with a short enough curve or long enough incline so the grip car could coast to the pick-up point.

With a pull curve, the grip did not release the cable. Here, the cable was guided around the curve by a series of small, horizontal pulleys. Chafing bars above and outside the pulleys kept the grip holding the cable safely away from the pulleys. This new technology vastly increased the cable car's potential since it allowed lines to be installed along curved routes and regardless of topography.

Almost as complicated as curves were cable car crossings, an engineer's challenge and a gripman's nightmare. The moving cables had to be kept from touching each other and were built on two planes, with the older cable in the privileged higher plane. (Seniority determined superiority.)

Intersections were so tricky to build and operate that transit companies often went out of their way to avoid crossing one cable line with another. The gripman on the route with the lower cable had to let go of his cable well before reaching the crossing so that his cable would not touch the other cable. Otherwise, components could be crimped or damaged, fouling the entire mechanism and shutting down the line. More importantly, the gripman had to be sure his grip did not cut the other cable. An underground vault would be built at crossings to ensure that the carrying rollers, pulleys, sheaves, chafing bars and yokes meshed precisely.

Chicago's horse-drawn and cable lines were built to "standard" railroad gauge (four feet and eight and a half inches between the two rails). This allowed companies and lines to interchange equipment. Thus, a horse could pull a horsecar or a cable car on either horsecar or cable car tracks. Meanwhile, a grip car could pull a cable car trailer, horsecar or electric trolley car on cable car tracks.

THE POWERHOUSE

One reason the cable car technology was successful is that it spearheaded and exploited a transformation to centralized power generation. Before cable traction arrived on the transit scene, each transit car or train had its own source of power, whether a horse, battery, small steam locomotive or something else. With cable traction, power was generated remotely more efficiently. Transit companies built big centralized power plants, "noble giants…who day after day take valiantly up their endless task" of moving cable cars relatively inexpensively.

Chicago boasted thirteen such power plants housing boilers, engines and winding machinery that drove the cables. These massive plants were impressive signs of a new age and sometimes open for tours. Their "heart throbs are felt miles distant and propel the cables on their endless journeys," one engineer said. They were typically located near the line they served, ideally at a central location where they could power cables running in different directions. Each Chicago plant powered one to five cables.

Boilers burned coal or oil to create steam that powered stationary engines. The engines turned shafts that spun huge powered sheaves wound two or three times with cable in a figure eight or S pattern to prevent slippage. Maintaining a steady cable speed was difficult since the number of trains each cable pulled at any given time varied tremendously. Therefore, large flywheels were used to keep output smooth and consistent. CCR used sixty-five-ton flywheels, twenty-five feet in diameter.

Above: Inside one of Chicago's cable car powerhouses showing cables and winding machinery.

Opposite: A crew poses in front of an engine inside NCSR's powerhouse at Lincoln and Wrightwood Avenues in 1902. The man in the three-piece suit sitting in the swivel chair is probably the engineer. These powerhouses made Chicago's polluted air even dirtier by burning coal and oil. *Chicago History Museum*.

A tension mechanism, including carriages and weights, kept the cable tight. Slack was dangerous because it could push the cable out of position, allowing it to buckle, crimp or become entangled in the grip. Slack resulted from a natural stretching of the cable that could add five hundred feet to its length or from short-term factors, such as hot weather and the gripping and releasing of cars.

Surprisingly, most engines delivered only from 200 to 1,500 horsepower, at least initially. The fact that such a small amount of power was easily capable of moving the heavy cable and, say, fifteen cable cars carrying more than 1,200 people, all of which added up to more than two hundred tons, was a mechanical marvel. Today, many automobiles use over 300 horsepower to move one person.

The top speed was considered 14.00 miles per hour because at higher speeds friction between the cable and grip could produce enough heat to set the interior hemp rope afire. In one experiment, CCR found that the outer strands of a cable crystallized and broke at 14.75 miles per hour.

Powerhouses often included company offices or headquarters. Many of them also stored cars and housed the horses that moved cable cars into, out of and around the facility. As companies added cable lines, they were required to add equipment to their powerhouses. By 1892, in time for the World's Columbian Exposition, CCR's powerhouse at 21st and State Streets had ten boilers aggregating 2,800 horsepower and six engines aggregating 3,900 horsepower to pull five cables for two cable lines.

Still, cable car technology was considered inefficient because 40 to 60 percent of the power generated in the plant was needed to keep the cable itself moving rather than to move payload, i.e., cars and passengers. A study in 1888 estimated that 57 percent of the power generated was devoted to moving cables, 39 percent to moving cars and only 4 percent to moving passengers. Another study in 1894 determined that CCR could drive its 22,316-foot cable on Cottage Grove Avenue between 39th and 55th Streets with an expenditure of 382 horsepower. One cable car added only 8 horsepower to the expenditure.

Cable car powerhouses were sturdy buildings, and cable car infrastructure was durable, as demonstrated by a cyclone in St. Louis in 1896. It caused havoc in the city and removed the roof of the cable car powerhouse at Park Avenue and 18th Street but did not seriously damage the machinery. Remarkably, the cable line was restored to service the following day.

The Cars

Railcar terms mean different things to different people. The following definitions will be used throughout this book:

- streetcar: any transit car used on a street railway;
- horsecar: a streetcar pulled by a horse;
- cable car: a streetcar in a train powered by a continuously moving cable;
- grip car: a cable car equipped with a mechanism for gripping and releasing a cable;
- trailer: a streetcar pulled by another streetcar through no force of its own; and
- trolley: a streetcar powered by electricity delivered through overhead wires.

This grip car with reversible seats could travel in either direction. The jerky motion of cable traction led to much wear and tear, especially on top of the posts to which the roof was attached, as can be seen here. Cable cars required more body repairs and depreciated more quickly than other types of transit vehicles. *Railroad and Heritage Museum of Temple, Texas; LeRoy O. King Collection.*

Cable cars came in a variety of sizes, shapes and styles. Early grip cars were small, open vehicles about sixteen to nineteen feet long, six to eight feet wide and ten feet high. These cars seated twenty passengers and cost about $625 to $1,000. Early cable trailers were converted horsecars about twenty-nine feet long with seating for thirty passengers. Open trailers cost about $850, and closed trailers cost about $1,250. Initially, many street railways built their own cable cars, but soon they were buying specially built cable cars from railway car builders.

Over time, the cars got larger and more comfortable. Early cars had one four-wheel "truck" (set of wheels) in the center, something that made them bouncy and unstable. Later cars had two trucks, one at either end, providing a smoother ride. Large combination cars featured seats in a front open section, where the grip mechanism was located, and more seats in a rear enclosed section. They had forty to fifty seats and cost about $2,000 each.

A typical closed cable car trailer. Roofs were made of glass windows and hardwood covered with canvas. *Railroad and Heritage Museum of Temple, Texas; LeRoy O. King Collection.*

Chicago's cable car companies maintained two fleets of trailers: open cars for warm weather and closed cars for the winter. Due to double fleets, there might have been as many as seven hundred grips and two thousand trailers available for cable service. A coal- or wood-burning stove heated some closed cars, and conductors were known to scrounge for wood along the route to try to warm their car. Oil lamps provided minimal light internally. Grip cars had large portable oil headlights that illuminated the way or at least provided pedestrians a warning that a train was approaching.

Chicago's cable cars had two kinds of brakes. Wheel brakes had iron pads that pressed against each wheel and were operated with a pedal, lever or handle, depending on the car type. On one-truck cars, the gripman operated the wheel brakes; on two-truck cars, the gripman operated the front wheel brakes while the conductor operated the rear wheel brakes.

Track brakes consisted of long blocks of pinewood located on the trucks between the wheels. They were operated by the gripman with a large lever located next to the grip lever. Pulling back on the lever forced the blocks of wood against the rails. Soft wood was used because it provided better friction than hard wood. On the other hand, the soft wood burned slightly with each application and needed to be replaced every few days.

CHAPTER 2

THE CABLE CAR EXPERIENCE

WHAT WAS IT LIKE TO RIDE ON A CABLE CAR IN CHICAGO?

Initially, passengers were excited by the prospect of riding on transit's newest conveyance and pleased with the experience. Cable cars were larger than horsecars, and the ride was smoother and more comfortable. And the twelve- or even fourteen-mile-per-hour speed was the fastest that many people had ever traveled, certainly through city streets. That must have been exhilarating.

"A morning ride on a cable-car is as pleasant and invigorating as can be imagined, and when the warm winds of summer have given place to snow and cold, there are still a large number who religiously occupy their favored seats on the grip-car and, well wrapped, take a health-giving constitutional on their way to business every morning," one contemporary wrote.

Often, people rode the cable cars solely for entertainment or amusement, that account continued. "Even the wealthy owner of the finest equipage is glad to let his hansom horses rest in their stalls while he indulges in the pleasures of a ride on the grip [car]."

The cable car was also an interesting curiosity. Residents and visitors alike did not know what to make of the new contraption. "They are not pulled by horses, neither do they work with steam or any other outside means of traction," wrote Frenchman L. de Cotton in his diary of a visit to Chicago in 1886. "I visited the machines that work hundreds of these cars and I must confess that I did not understand completely the mystery of the mechanism."

Children assemble for a "health giving constitutional" ride on a "fresh-air transit outing," circa 1902. *Chicago History Museum.*

After a few years, however, riders became disenchanted with cable cars. The poorly heated cars were cold in the winter, and the open summer cars provided scant protection from the rain—only a dropdown cloth curtain at the end of each row of seats. Since trains could not pass each other, they tended to bunch together, adding to overall street congestion. If the gripman grabbed the cable too quickly, riders got a jolt. Complaints about slow service, breakdowns, accidents and overcrowding became common. Most of these disadvantages had been somewhat true with horsecars, but the improved features of cable traction had begun to raise people's expectations—a trend that eventually led to improved streets, expressways and the diminishment of transit.

The poor found the mandated five-cent fare steep, but workers and members of the middle class could readily pay the fare. Increasingly, passengers complained that the ride was not worth a nickel while transit companies insisted that riders were getting a good deal, especially as the city grew.

Passengers also complained about transfer policies, even though such policies were more generous in Chicago than in most other cities. Street railways experimented with myriad transfer policies with various time limitations, points of issue and color-coded tickets. Some riders became confused while others flouted the rules and gave or sold their transfers to boys who resold them. Conductors, too, could be tempted to collude with shopkeepers and others and to share in the take. Eventually, streetcar managements began numbering transfers before releasing them to conductors.

The North and West Side transit companies angered the public for initially not allowing transfers on their cable lines. Invariably, "the unwary passenger gets the hot end of the proceedings," an editorial said. Another newspaper reported in 1895 that passengers were unhappy at not being allowed to transfer between West Side cable cars and North Side horsecars, even when through-cars from both companies were coupled in the same cable train and Chicago Cable Car Czar Yerkes owned both companies.

There were many obscure fare policies, too. By day, a passenger could ride the entire length of CCR's Cottage Grove Avenue cable line to Hyde Park or Oak Woods for a nickel. At night, however, the same trip required two fares: one on the Cottage Grove Avenue night horsecar to 39th Street and another on the Hyde Park night horsecar. That rule made sense to CCR, although the company quietly dropped the policy after a high-profile situation involving a prominent judge as a passenger.

ഇ)⊘

Cable car accidents occurred infrequently and were rarely fatal. When they did occur, few if any people were injured, primarily due to the cable car's slow speed as well as passengers' tendency to jump from cars when they anticipated danger. Although exciting back in the day, cable speeds were relatively slow, and the cars were light in weight, so the destructive energy produced in a mishap was small compared to that of an automobile crash today.

A typical accident was described in the December 14, 1888 *Hyde Park Herald*: "Mrs. Thos Otis was thrown from the cable car last Saturday by the sudden starting of the car and very severely bruised. She will be confined to the house for some weeks."

Since it took thirty to eighty tons of tension to sever a cable, cables rarely broke except in cold weather on lines with many curves. (This happened frequently, for example, in Grand Rapids, Michigan, but rarely in Chicago.) Even when a cable broke, it did not do much damage or cause injuries. A break did, however, shut down an entire line for several hours or however long it took to fish the two ends of the broken cable out of the conduit and make a temporary splice.

Although cables rarely broke, the grip occasionally became entangled in a loose strand of the cable, causing the train to smash through obstacles, unable to stop even by braking. The gripman with the entangled grip would ring his bell furiously in warning, and a nonstop parade of trains in front would race along, trying to stay ahead of the runaway train to avoid being pushed along, derailed or crushed. In 1888, the *Railroad Gazette* reported:

> *A grip car beyond control and running at the rate of eight miles per hour…caused a lively scene in Chicago one night last week. The result was three badly wrecked cars, many frightened women and children, and some severe contusions, but no fatalities. As a Clark Street [train] came out of the tunnel on LaSalle [Street] going south, the driver applied the brakes, but without effect, as a strand of cable had wrapped itself around the grip, and the grip would not release. Just ahead of this was a Wells Street train filled with passengers. At Monroe Street, the Wells Street train was struck and thrown into a gutter.*

A similar runaway train caused a spectacular group of collisions along several blocks of Madison Street in 1892, derailing or damaging six trains. Although the trains were crowded, no one was killed or hurt badly enough to require hospitalization.

The only way to bring a runaway train to a halt was to stop the cable and untangle the broken strand from the grip. Some lines in Chicago installed trackside alarm boxes so the conductor could signal the powerhouse when a cable strand became entangled. Other lines installed broken-strand detectors that sounded an alarm in the powerhouse. In the absence of such devices, the conductor on a runaway train had to jump off the moving train and seek a telephone to call the powerhouse.

Disasters caused by a ruptured cable or broken strand occurred less frequently after the introduction in 1880 of open-hearth steel production, which made cables stronger and more reliable.

A disproportionate number of accidents occurred on the downtown loops along Wabash Avenue, LaSalle Street and State Street, where cable cars operated on the left side of the street, contrary to the flow of traffic. With pull curves that took trains around busy corners at the full speed of the cable, downtown loops accounted for one of the worst operating conditions cable traction ever presented.

WORLD'S FAIR SERIES NO. 8.

THE
GRAPHIC
CHICAGO

VOL. VIII, No. 11.   CHICAGO, MARCH 18, 1893.   SUBSCRIPTION, $4.00 PER YEAR.   TEN CENTS PER COPY.

Although infrequent, cable car accidents were most often caused by a loose strand of the cable getting caught in the grip. This dragged the train along the track until it ran into something or crashed. *Chicago History Museum.*

Accidents, even fatalities, occurred more frequently in or near the downtown tunnels with their relatively steep approaches and exits. On August 29, 1890, gripman Frank Metzger was killed when his train hit a derailed car on a runaway train coming the other direction in the Washington Street tunnel. On December 11, 1894, two passengers died when a Milwaukee Avenue cable train entering the Washington Street tunnel smashed into the train ahead. On February 15, 1900, a train was pushing a disabled train out of a tunnel when the rear platform of that train's back trailer collapsed from the pressure.

A lesser problem in the tunnels was flooding. On September 3, 1894, heavy rains closed the tunnels under Washington and Van Buren Streets. The former reopened quickly, although passengers had to stand on their seats as the cars rode through a few feet of water.

Because cable cars were so quiet, sometimes pedestrians accustomed to listening for the sound of horseshoes on pavement did not hear them coming. Henrietta Voss, whom the *New York Times* described as "recently arrived from a Michigan Village," died in 1898 after stepping in front of a cable car on Blue Island Avenue. This type of accident prompted some cable lines to put bells on the axles of their cars, adding to the cable car cacophony of humming cables, ringing fare registers and clanging gongs.

Street railways adopted various types of fenders and wheel guards to push unwary pedestrians aside, lift them off the tracks or at least prevent limbs from being severed by the car's unforgiving wheels. Some fenders included a net of rope or steel spring tines to hold the hapless victim above the tracks until the gripman could stop the car. Such appliances led to unintended consequences, as reported in the *Washington Bee* in 1901 and posted on the extremely informative site www.cable-car-guy.com. A tired Michael Nolan "yearned for a nice, soft spot on which to rest his weary bones. He was not particular where he rested himself or the kind of a bed he chose." Nolan lay down on the fender of a Madison Street cable car stopped at Desplaines Street and fell asleep. After being spotted, "he felt indignant at being disturbed." He was taken to jail and fined five dollars the next morning.

The rails, slots and flat metal hatches on the street along cable lines formed hazards for pedestrians, drivers and horses. A horseshoe calk caught in the slot could injure the horse if the shoe was pulled off. Bicyclists were at risk, too. On March 12, 1895, George Cohen was killed while cycling at Halsted and O'Brien Streets after his wheel slipped and he fell in front of a cable train.

Like horsecars before them, cable cars provided a ready excuse for being late to work. People blamed cable cars for other problems too. When Cornelius Corcoran killed two of his children and then himself in November 1899, the incident was attributed to an injury from a cable car collision three years earlier that had supposedly affected his brain.

Cable car companies also played the blame game. Many passengers were hurt boarding or exiting moving trains, but such accidents "are due in fully 99 percent of cases rather to excuseless and needless risks taken by the passenger than to any fault of the system or employees operating it," CCR claimed. Nonetheless, gripmen usually did not come to a full stop for able-bodied men to board or exit their train; typically, they stopped only for crowds, the elderly, the frail and ladies.

There is evidence but no documentation that smoking was prohibited on closed cable cars and permitted on open cars. Women tended to sit in the closed cars to avoid the smoke, as well as the wind—and perhaps the men.

Thieves and pickpockets on cable cars were all too common. In 1896, five men boarded a State Street cable car, blocked the exits, robbed several passengers and escaped. On another occasion, however, a cable car ride solved a residential burglary when a woman spotted a fellow passenger wearing a dress that had recently been stolen from her home. She had the woman arrested and recovered her dress.

Less harmful shenanigans involved boys who attached tin cans to a rope or wire that they dropped into the slot. If the cable engaged the rope or wire, the cans would clatter along the street. Rowdier boys would attach a wagon, box or washbasin to the rope or wire before lowering it through the slot. With a bit of luck, they got a wild ride—at least until the conductor or police chased them away.

Overall, the streets were cleaner thanks to cable cars, but the air was dirtier due to the pollution created by burning coal and oil in powerhouses, which were typically located downtown or in residential areas.

What Was It Like to Work for a Cable Car Line?

In the 1880s, transit jobs were highly sought. The work was steady, the pay decent and the conditions tolerable, sometimes even enjoyable, especially compared to the alternatives. Gripmen and experienced conductors earned about nineteen cents an hour; by 1906, that had risen to about thirty cents an hour. Most of the men on the cars worked ten to twelve hours a day six or seven days a week. Some worked years without a day off. In any event, there were always more men willing to work than positions available.

The development of the cable car created a new class of skilled worker: the gripman. He had to be strong, "not a panty-waist" in the words of a contemporary writer. If anything or anyone got in the way of a moving car, the gripman had to hit the obstacle or bring his car to a sudden stop. To accomplish this, the gripman would sometimes have to pull back on the grip or brake with the force of 125 pounds. Other times he would hold his grip in his fingertips like a tuning fork to detect the carrying rollers, pulleys and bars hidden underground that issued his "operating instructions" through rubs, taps and vibrations.

"The gripman who controlled the cable train became the envy of small boys admiring his strength in manipulating tall levers…knowing when to grip the cable, when to coast and when to drop the cable from the grip," said James J. Buckley and Roy G. Benedict in their authoritative yet unpublished typescript, "Chicago's West Division Street Railways in the 1800s."

Although traveling around the city, wearing a uniform and interacting with the public must have been better than working in the stockyards or shoveling coal, the work was not for everyone. Companies enforced militaristic discipline, and inspectors kept a sharp eye on workers. On most cars, gripmen had no protection from the cold in the winter, other than a massive coat. The "buffalo" coat made of bison hair was popular. Meanwhile, conductors had their hands full dealing with increasingly dissatisfied passengers.

If a conductor or gripman missed his run, he went back to the bottom of the seniority ladder, where he would be given assignments sporadically and at off hours. But the ultimate infraction was for a gripman to cut the cable at a let-go point by failing to handle the grip correctly. This resulted in immediate dismissal.

Conductors were notorious for skimming money—even though they carried registers to count passengers and had to account for their registered fares at the end of each day. Sometimes gripmen colluded with conductors. Such a team would run their train slowly to pick up a more-than-usual number of passengers and pocket some fares without registering them. Due to the extra passengers,

Exposed to the elements all day, gripmen had a tough, physically demanding job, as seen in this drawing of a Chicago gripman from the cover of *Harper's Weekly*, February 25, 1893.

they would still be able to hand in average revenues and thereby avoid detection. Company employees called "spotters," sometimes posing as passengers, attempted to detect such malfeasance. An adverse report from a spotter typically meant dismissal of the conductor.

Less in the public view, other categories of workers kept things running. By day, an engineer and a team of firemen in the powerhouse tended the engines that drove the cables. By night, skilled cable splicers inspected and repaired the cable while it was shut down. Other workers oiled and serviced the grips and replaced brake shoes as needed.

The conduit required continual maintenance. Workers cleaned the conduit by sweeping out debris through the slot and climbing into the hatches and vaults to scrape out muck. Cable lines had a series of metal hatches on the street to allow workers to lubricate and maintain the cable. Other workers lubricated track components, including the carrying rollers. CCR averaged 330 carrying rollers per mile of double track, and each one had to be lubricated by lifting access plates along the right-of-way. This was a tricky job since an over-lubricated cable would slip through the grip. It took an "oil refinery" and four men working constantly to keep one of Chicago's cable lines operating, an industry official commented.

When the slot closed up, crews used sledgehammers and wedges to force it open so the shank holding the grip could move freely through the slot. During the winter of 1894–95, the slot on the Blue Island Avenue line narrowed so much that several trains derailed. Even this late in the development of cable traction, designing yokes that would maintain a constant slot width despite seasonal changes in temperature and soil pressure was an inexact science.

Other workers staffed wreck wagons around the clock to deal with derailments, collisions, broken-down wagons blocking the tracks or a dead workhorse too heavy for bystanders to roll off the tracks. A few seconds after a call, "a fine team may be seen dashing out of the car house to the scene of the blockade…making as good time as the Fire Department," read an 1887 CCR souvenir booklet. The wreck wagon was "equipped with tools of all kinds, bars, levers, powerful jack-screws, blocks and tackles, saws, sledges, cutting tools, chains, axes, timbers, nuts of assorted sizes…extra wagon wheels…and a clanging gong."

In December 1894, a grip broke on a three-car, westbound train at Clinton Street as it was leaving the Washington Street tunnel. The train slid backward and derailed the train behind it. The wreck wagon crew cleaned up the debris and returned the follower to the rails. (Cable cars were so light that men using large levers could often lift a car back onto the track.) Then the follower pushed the disabled train out of the tunnel and back to the car barn.

A CCR cable train said to be located at Cable Court and Lake (now Lake Park) Avenue. Mark Harris, the conductor on the left, was born in Manchester, England, worked on the cable car for about fifteen years and then opened a saloon shortly after this photo was taken, circa 1900. *Crerar Library, University of Chicago.*

Bridge wagons were also kept ready. A fire hose laid across tracks would shut down a cable line for the duration of a fire and cleanup. Therefore, portable bridges were used to hold hoses above tracks. They had thirteen-foot-high trestles shaped like inverted Vs with rods laid horizontally across the top. Up to five hoses could be held on each bridge. Alerted by the city's fire alarm system, the lightweight, horse-drawn bridge wagon could usually get to a fire before the crew of a heavily loaded fire wagon had set up its hoses.

Cable cars usually continued to operate in the snow, powering their way through even deep snow thanks to the force of the steam engines driving them. "On more than one occasion when every steam railroad entering the city was unable to turn a wheel, the cable cars were running as usual without the loss of a single trip," CCR boasted. "Its tracks afforded the only means of travel for pedestrians and the only path for teams."

Ice was a more serious problem. In 1904, the *Chicago Tribune* reported that a broken water main flooded the conduit under Halsted Street. The water froze and snapped the cable.

Transit companies claimed that cable cars made good snowplows. The cars did clear a path for other vehicles and pedestrians, but residents objected that they simply pushed the snow aside into the street. *Chicago Public Library, Special Collections and Preservation Division.*

ഔ

As good as cable car jobs were compared to many other jobs, conditions were often rough, and workers faced long hours, split shifts and strict work rules. Sometimes they addressed their concerns through negotiations. Many cable car employees belonged to quasi unions or worker associations that represented them. One of the more prominent such groups was the Knights of Labor, more of an order than a union, although it occasionally negotiated with management on behalf of its members.

The relationship between labor and management in Chicago during the 1880s and 1890s was submissive at best and violent at worst. Prompted by CCR's threat to cut conductors' wages, Chicago's first cable car strike occurred in 1883. When gripmen walked off in support, the strike brought the South Side lines to a standstill. Some cars were derailed, and some replacement crews were "speedily brought to grief" by the disgruntled workers, said the *New York Times*. The strike ended after a couple of days when the conductors were guaranteed their old rates, prompting the men to hold "a jollification meeting over their victory."

Labor-management relations went from bad to worse after the Haymarket Square bombing in 1886 and subsequent hangings of supposed anarchists in 1887. Chicago's most serious cable car strike occurred the following year starting on the North Side. Workers objected to long, irregular hours, heavy security deposits for punches and exorbitant charges for uniforms made by the company tailor. They also asked to be paid by the trip rather than by the hour; for a maximum number of work hours per day; and for nondiscriminatory treatment of union workers. And gripmen and conductors wanted their wages raised from an average of nineteen to twenty-seven cents an hour.

Following advice from a local leader of the Knights, workers met with Yerkes in the summer of 1888. Stridently anti-union, Yerkes dug in. After no progress was made, five hundred North Chicago Street Railroad (NCSR) employees went on strike. On October 6, Yerkes blamed professional agitators and vowed to fight, having already brought in three hundred workers from Kansas City, Pittsburgh and Philadelphia. All of these cities had cable cars, so these could have been experienced workers. On October 8, NCSR resumed service using horsecars. Police protected the cars, but few passengers rode because the public supported the strikers.

Saying that the strike was costing the city $1 million a day, Mayor John A. Roche intervened. When his efforts failed to resolve the issues, 1,300 employees of Yerkes's vast West Chicago Street Railroad joined the strike.

A few days later, working on behalf of Yerkes, the police accused a worker of having dynamite. In fact, he had "track torpedoes," harmless noise-making devices that were

A two-week strike against CCR in 1903 led to violence and arrests. Here, police guard a cable train headed to Jackson Park. *Chicago History Museum.*

clamped to the top of the rail to signal a locomotive engineer when to stop. Raising the specter of dynamite turned public opinion against the strikers. More negotiations resolved the strike on October 15. Gripmen saw their wages increase from $2.75 to $2.90 a day and conductors theirs from $2.50 to $2.65. In addition, the workday was set at no fewer than ten but no more than twelve hours.

Despite these gains, Yerkes outsmarted the men. He retained more than two hundred of the imported workers, all of whom had signed contracts prohibiting union membership. This crippled union efforts to organize the workers. In 1898, a City Council committee found no unions among Chicago's three major streetcar companies. "Charles had succeeded in creating a docile workforce," John Franch wrote in *Robber Baron*, his thorough and highly readable biography of Yerkes.

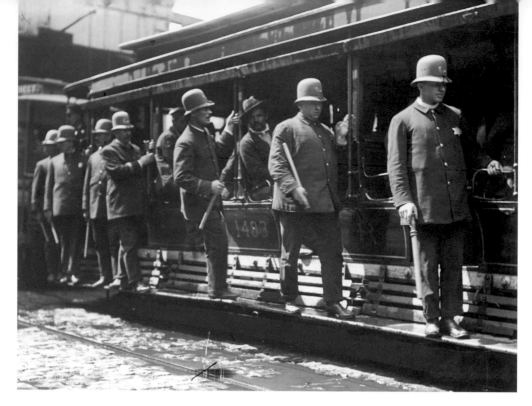

During many strikes, there were more police riding the trains than passengers. The public stayed away out of sympathy for the strikers and/or fear of violence. *Chicago History Museum.*

Many workers felt that Republican Mayor Roche had deceived them and connived with Yerkes. He was targeted in the next election and lost to pro-labor Dewitt Clinton Cregier, a Democrat.

Another strike occurred in 1900 when CCR's powerhouse employees walked out, but their action was ineffective as CCR quickly replaced them with other workers.

CCR's trainmen went on strike in 1903. The trainmen asked for higher wages, shorter hours and a closed, all-union shop. When the company ran cable trains on Cottage Grove Avenue and trolleys on Wentworth Avenue, mobs wrecked several cars, injured a dozen men and plugged the slot. On the second day, firemen and engineers who worked in cable car powerhouses joined the strike but were quickly replaced.

Violence continued for days, and many arrests were made. Police escorted trains, many of which carried more police than passengers. Stones and timbers were placed on tracks, and rocks were thrown at police and passengers from the tops of buildings. Scabs risked injury. CCR hired six hundred Pinkerton detectives but continued to have difficulty operating trains. Other unionized workers—cable splicers, electricians, machinists and shopmen—joined the strike, but to little avail. The strike ended after two weeks. Work hours were curtailed, and the union and company agreed to negotiate wages, but the shop remained open to nonunion workers.

CHAPTER 3

BEFORE CABLE CARS: HORSE POWER

Prior to the introduction of cable cars, early transit technologies varied tremendously—from practical to impractical, successful to unsuccessful, brilliant to foolish. Overlapping in time and place, many of these technologies competed with each other. Invariably built by private enterprise, they were driven by the desire to make a profit, even if only a nickel at a time.

THE OMNIBUS

Historians consider New York's horse-drawn omnibus, which debuted in 1827, the country's first transit line. "Omnibus" comes from Latin for "all" (and was later shortened to "bus"). Running 1¾ miles on Broadway, this four-wheel carriage had open sides and seated twelve passengers in two compartments. Riders signaled their desire to disembark by pulling a leather strap attached to the driver's ankle. The brainchild of enterprising hackney-operator Abraham Brower, this modest forerunner of America's vast urban transit industry was invitingly called *Accommodation*.

In 1829, Brower added a second vehicle called *Sociable*, probably because it had longitudinal seating, with riders facing each other across the center aisle of a single compartment. As the name *Sociable* implied, the omnibus was remarkable for creating a new public space that thrust diverse city dwellers together, both physically and socially. Within a few years, Brower had more than one hundred imitators along Manhattan's rutted streets.

Following New York's example, other cities inaugurated omnibus service, including Philadelphia in 1831 and Boston in 1835. Nevertheless, the shortcomings of this primitive form of transit far outweighed its benefits. Its large, spindly wheels made the coaches hard to enter and exit, and the ride was loud, uncomfortable and bumpy. In 1864, the *New York Herald* was one of many papers to criticize the omnibus, calling a ride in one a modern mode of "martyrdom." "The driver quarrels with the passengers. There are quarrels about getting on and getting off. There are quarrels about change and quarrels about the ticket swindle. The driver swears at the passenger and the passengers harangue the driver. Thus the omnibus rolls along, a veritable bedlam on wheels."

CHICAGO'S OMNIBUSES

Omnibuses began to appear sporadically in Chicago in the late 1840s after livery stable operator Samuel Walker apparently launched Chicago's first significant omnibus service. In 1850, another livery stable operator, Warren Parker, began providing omnibuses on State, Madison and Clark Streets, and others also entered the business.

Omnibus service developed hand-in-glove with the growth of intercity passenger train lines. The several railroads that began operating in Chicago in the early 1850s were not allowed to build their stations in the city center. This created long, sometimes arduous transfers for passengers between stations or to hotels, restaurants and businesses. Some stations, hotels and stores provided transfer services, but the new omnibus companies aggressively targeted this business.

Profitable for their operators, omnibuses were never popular in Chicago because the ride was rough and slow. This was due to the condition of Chicago's dusty or muddy streets as much as to the boxy design of the omnibus. During this time, Chicago's streets "were in a condition which rendered travel vexatious and perilous to both man and beast," said the 1895 *History of Chicago*. Only a narrow center section of State Street downtown was paved, and that was with loosely laid wooden planks. After it rained, the mud under the planks would squirt up when a wagon passed, muddying passengers and pedestrians alike. And if an omnibus slipped off the plank road, it could take hours to pull it out of the mud.

Omnibus owners were a competitive, entrepreneurial lot. Most famed among them was Franklin Parmelee, a former stagecoach driver and steamship crewman. In 1852, he bought out Parker, for whom he worked. He proceeded to buy out the omnibuses of several leading hotels and came to dominate the transfer business. By 1886, his company employed eighty omnibuses, seventy baggage wagons, 250 horses and two hundred men.

Fares settled in at five cents and created a transit standard that would prevail for decades. Too much for poor or working people to pay, this fare was mainly affordable to members of the middle class. The rich likely had their own buggies or could afford to hire taxis for thirty to fifty cents or horse and carriages for, say, three dollars a day.

Ultimately, Chicago's street railways drove the plodding omnibuses out of business, although a few omnibuses continued to operate in Chicago until the early twentieth century. Parmelee's company evolved into Continental Airport Express, which transfers more than one million passengers a year to and from Chicago's airports.

Horse-Drawn Street Railways

The next type of transit to develop was the horse-drawn street railway. Running on rails, the ride was smoother but limited to a fixed route. Horsecars provided the public increased convenience and comfort but negligible savings in transit times because the poky cars traveled about five miles per hour, only slightly faster than a person could walk.

What is recognized as the first street railway in the United States, and likely the world, came about somewhat by accident. The line was built by the New York & Harlem Railroad (NY&H), which was incorporated not as a street railway but rather as a conventional intercity steam railroad. The NY&H used its intercity railroad authorization to build a short street railway as a "feeder" line to carry customers to the proposed southern terminal of its intercity railroad. Completing this horse-drawn feeder line before finishing its intercity steam railroad, the NY&H began to operate the street railway line on its own in 1832.

The one-mile service started with two new horsecars, each of which could seat thirty passengers inside with overflow seating on the roof, inaugurating a seating style that survived, formally or otherwise, around the country well into the twentieth

Following pages: The omnibus was Chicago's first form of transit. One is still operating here (lower left) in 1905. Meanwhile, a cable train heads south, contrary to the flow of traffic, on the left side of State Street at Washington Street. This grip car with reversible seats and control levers in the middle of the car could operate in either direction. *Chicago Transit Authority.*

century. The carefully designed and well-decorated cars were novel enough that they warranted a patent. At that time, the size of the federal government was so small that President Andrew Jackson personally signed the patent for the NY&H's horsecars.

New York's populace turned out in great numbers to witness the launch of the new horsecar service. "Groups of spectators greeted the passengers of the cars with shouts, and every window in the Bowery was filled," said the *Morning Courier and New-York Enquirer*. New York Mayor Walter Bowne was so impressed with the service that he proclaimed, "This event will go down in the history of our country as the greatest achievement of man."

Other street railways entered the fray, and horsecars became increasingly crowded. In 1865, the *New York Herald* grumbled, "The seats being more than filled, the passengers are placed in rows down the middle, where they hang on by the straps, like smoked hams in a corner grocery."

Still, horsecars were slow to catch on outside of New York. Few other cities were big enough to warrant any kind of transit. New Orleans built a horsecar line in 1835, but that was it until lines were built in Brooklyn (1853); Boston/Cambridge (1856); Philadelphia (1858); and Baltimore, St. Louis, Pittsburgh, Cincinnati and, finally, Chicago (1859). By the mid-1880s, however, the horsecar was a fixture in nearly every American city of any significant size.

Typically, eight to ten horses were needed per railcar: two at a time to pull the car in three- or four-hour shifts, depending on the load, with some horses held in reserve for emergencies, transferring cars in the car barn and other work. Thomas Edison called them the poorest motor ever employed, yielding a thermal efficiency of only 2 percent.

ᔆᗠᘔ

Although most people think of the American Society for the Prevention of Cruelty to Animals (ASPCA) as an organization dedicated to the welfare of cats and dogs, it was founded in 1866 specifically to protect workhorses. Its founder, wealthy New Yorker Henry Bergh, devoted much of his life to saving horses from abuse. Many horses in transit service were severely overworked. Nags judged no longer fit for service were often released into the street to starve, and carcasses of dead horses along city streets were a common sight. Some heralded cable cars as a way to relieve such abuse.

For his part, Bergh lobbied for laws to punish cruelty to animals. He organized and led a force of inspectors to patrol the streets of New York and eventually other cities, as seen in this item from ASPCA annals: "New York City, April 1866. The driver of a cart laden with coal is whipping his horse. Passersby…stop to gawk not so much at

Henry Bergh founded the American Society for the Prevention of Cruelty to Animals to protect workhorses. Here, he intervenes on behalf of abused horses pulling an overcrowded streetcar in an 1872 drawing from *Harper's Weekly*. *New York Public Library.*

the weak, emaciated equine, but at the tall man [Bergh], elegant in top hat and spats and special badge, who is explaining to the driver that it is now against the law to beat one's animal."

Later, Bergh took on dog fighting and other canine causes. In 1867, he helped pass a law that prohibited the use of dogs to pull carts without a license. With a flair for drama, Bergh once dropped in on a dogfight through a skylight, thereby disrupting and publicizing the illegal event. As cable cars, electric trolleys and motorized vehicles replaced workhorses, ASPCA changed its focus to protecting other animals, particularly cats and dogs.

CHICAGO'S HORSE-DRAWN STREET RAILWAYS

In 1850, Chicago was a frontier outpost with 29,963 inhabitants, the nation's twenty-fourth most populous city. Ten years later, it had grown to 112,177 inhabitants, the nation's ninth most populous city. Chicago was ready for transit.

It was the entrepreneurial omnibus operator Parmelee who led Chicago into the street railway era. He quickly discovered, however, that running horsecars was entirely different than running omnibuses. Street railways were heavily regulated, entrenched in politics and subject to public opinion.

In 1859, the state legislature incorporated three street railways, one for each side of town, North, South and West, as divided by the Chicago River. These companies quickly built up an extensive network of lines, and Chicagoans took to horsecars in droves. Horsecar tickets even became used as currency. "These tickets were the most acceptable small change Chicago had," said the *History of Chicago*.

Chicago's standard horsecar seated twenty passengers, although up to ninety riders crammed into the small space during peak periods. Empty, the car weighed about four thousand pounds. When crowded, the two horses that typically pulled a horsecar would struggle with their load, which could top seven tons. Horsecars were lit by small oil lamps. They were not heated, but in the winter straw on the floor supposedly helped passengers keep their feet warm. In the summer, cars with open sides were used.

With its need for drivers, conductors, stablemen, blacksmiths, harness makers, car builders, painters, veterinarians and others, the new industry sparked the development of crafts and trades. Most of these men tended to work hard sixteen hours a day with one or no day off a week.

Street railways also sparked a booming business in bribery and corruption. The City Council had the right to approve routes and issue franchises. This was done through an ordinance, passed by the City Council and signed by the mayor. If the street railway accepted the conditions spelled out in the ordinance, it was granted a franchise to conduct business. Aldermen lined up to extort money from street railways by selling their approval of a proposed ordinance or by supporting favorable conditions for a franchise. Often they would play one applicant or railway against another. Many proposed lines and ordinances were designed for the sole purpose of forcing an existing street railway to pay off aldermen for blocking a potential competitor.

Since the law required approval of at least half of the property owners along each mile of a proposed route, private individuals got into the act as well. Property owners openly sold their consent—and often rescinded it later when they got a higher

A West Chicago Street Railroad horsecar at the Kedzie Avenue car barn in 1891. Billy Orr, on the left, is the driver and Chas Remer is the conductor.

price from another party opposing the proposed line. Such practices continued later throughout Chicago's cable car era.

Despite the high cost of bribes and payoffs, Chicago's horsecar companies generated steady dividends and returns. The lines were relatively inexpensive to build, especially in the beginning when companies would simply spike down rails on the city's plank roads. Nevertheless, horsecar lines were expensive to operate, with horses composing from one-third to two-thirds of a company's total costs. The strong, agile and calm horses needed to pull railcars through often chaotic street traffic were expensive to start with. Then it took two months for most horses to become accustomed to traffic and about a year to be considered seasoned. All along, they had to be fed, groomed and stabled. And transit service wore them out in just four to six years.

In addition to being expensive, horses were susceptible to illness and disease. In 1872, the Great Epizootic spread through eastern cities, killing thousands of horses and disabling thousands more. In Philadelphia, it killed 2,500 horses in three weeks, and in New York, it killed or incapacitated 18,000 horses.

Later that year, the disease reached Chicago, where it "spread like wildfire" through the city's population of approximately twenty-five thousand horses, according to the *Inter Ocean*. This left Chicago's usually crowded, hectic streets "as still as the streets of a suburb." Many horsecar lines suspended service, leaving residents "solely to their feet for locomotion," the article continued. "How dependent humanity is on horseflesh was never so apparent." Other transit lines continued operating by replacing horses with mules or hiring gangs of immigrants to pull streetcars.

The disease quickly ran its course, but the fact that horses created a huge sanitation problem in the rapidly growing city only intensified. By the 1880s, some seven thousand horses were pulling transit vehicles in Chicago. They dumped millions of pounds of manure and tens of thousands of gallons of urine on the streets each year. This was not only odiferous and unpleasant, but it also created health issues, the most serious of which was the tetanus virus carried in horse feces.

Despite all of these problems, horses continued to be the main form of motive power on Chicago's transit scene for many years, even after cable cars were introduced. By 1890, there were more than 150 miles of horsecar tracks in the city, with the average Chicagoan riding 164 times that year.

SEARCHING FOR AN ALTERNATIVE TO HORSES

Horse-powered transit had inherent limitations and serious shortcomings. Therefore, street railways, investors, civic organizations and the city doggedly, even desperately, sought alternatives. During the second half of the nineteenth century, everyone from tinkerers to transit titans experimented with mechanical forms of motive power. This was a period of great and varied experimentation. In 1887, Chicago City Railway claimed to have expended "large sums in experimenting through a series of years with almost every known device in the hope of securing something better than animal power."

Engineers and entrepreneurs launched one scheme after another through trial and error—primarily the latter. Some of these schemes were bizarre, some actually worked, but all of them seemed worth exploring at the time, at least to someone. They included devices on, below and above the ground powered by batteries; naphtha (a petroleum derivative); small steam locomotives; fireless steam locomotives that were recharged with super-heated water from stationary boilers along the line; compressed air, likewise recharged along the line; electricity from overhead or underground wires; ammonia gas; giant clockwork springs; flywheels; and even internal combustion engines.

A West Chicago Dummy Railway train. Such diminutive locomotives were called "dummies" due to efforts to mute their noise and exhausts. This one was named *Waldheim*. *Chicago Public Library, Special Collections and Preservation Division.*

Of the myriad and diverse proposals to replace the horse, "each for itself claims, if not perfection, certainly that it is better than any other system," said an author in 1888.

Early on, the most obvious alternative to horse-powered transit was the steam locomotive. Up until the 1880s, there were more attempts to harness steam than any other alternative. In the 1860s, street railways in Chicago experimented with small steam locomotives designed to look like horsecars. They were called "dummies," but it is not certain whether the term referred to efforts to mute the vehicles' noise and exhausts or to disguise their appearance so as to avoid spooking horses.

In 1867, the Chicago & Calumet Horse and Dummy Railroad began operating the region's first dummy railway in Hyde Park, then a suburb. Three other suburban transit companies followed suit, prompting the *Chicago Evening Journal* to proclaim in 1869 "another milestone in the path which is being cut through old fogy prejudices, and which will eventually lead to steam power on all of our street railways." As late as 1892, the steam locomotive was selected as the best way to power Chicago's new "L," the city's elevated rail transit system. The first two "L" lines used locomotives for a few years before converting to the trackside third-rail electrical system pioneered at the World's Columbian Exposition of 1893 and still used today.

Nevertheless, the steam locomotive was not the solution everyone sought. It was loud, dirty, accident prone and ill suited for stop-and-go service. More importantly, it did not offer a significant cost savings over horsecar operations.

Surrounded by steam-powered traction and myriad other competing street railway technologies, inventors and entrepreneurs also tested and refined cable traction systems using overhead, trackside and underground wire cables to pull vehicles. Their progress was slow, as we shall see, but they eventually held center stage for a couple of decades.

CHAPTER 4

CABLE CARS ARRIVE
ON THE SCENE

Due to the continued presence of cable cars in San Francisco and exaggerated claims regarding San Francisco's role in the origin of cable cars, many people believe that cable cars sprang into existence in the City by the Bay through a stroke of inventive genius on the part of one man. The legend holds that Andrew Hallidie conceived of cable cars one foggy day after witnessing a horsecar trying to make its way up a steep, slippery, San Francisco hill. When one of the horses fell, the car slid back down the hill, dragging the horses with it.

Whether this story is true, Hallidie has been coronated as the inventor. Various sources call him "the mechanical genius who originated cable railway transportation"; credit him with inventing "a brand new idea in city transportation"; and say, "all credit for producing a workable cable tramway must go to Hallidie."

In fact, the story of the origin of the cable car is much more complex and interesting. As George Hilton said in his definitive book, *The Cable Car in America*, attributing the cable car to Hallidie would be "on a par in accuracy with attributing the locomotive or the steamboat to an individual…Cable traction was a highly derivative invention, not only in drawing on a combination of existing technology but in having abundant precursors."

Prior to Hallidie's work with cable cars in San Francisco, underground or overhead wire and rope cables had long been used to move coal, ore, rock and debris in mines and quarries around the world. They had also been used to carry people and materials up and down steep inclines and across rivers. And as early as 1812, two inventors proposed moving vehicles on city streets by using a fixed cable with winding devices on the vehicles. A decade later, another inventor proposed pulling vehicles along roads using a chain in a hollow rail.

Cable car technology did not spring from one man's imagination. Rather, it had abundant predecessors. This photo shows two of CCR's original cable cars (a grip car and a trailer) photographed in 1881, shortly before the State Street cable line commenced operations. The trailer is a single-truck horsecar converted to cable service. *Chicago Transit Authority.*

In 1829, W. Dick proposed an endless cable traction system powered by a stationary power source. In 1838, W.H. Curtis applied for a patent for a quick-release gripper that foreshadowed the cable car grip. In 1845, E.W. Brandling proposed the first system based on a cable moving continuously in an open box that was reached by a gripping mechanism from the car. Zeroing in on the ultimate design, in 1858, E.S. Gardiner of Philadelphia applied for a patent for an underground conduit that included a narrow slot in the track for grabbing a continuously moving underground cable and was equipped with the means for guiding the cable on its path. Gardiner's work was so important that J. Bucknall Smith in his 1887 seminal *Treatise Upon Cable or Rope Traction* said, "It is fair to recognise [*sic*] that all cable haulage schemes at present in use for

street tramways have been constructed in accordance with the principles laid down by Gardiner. His designs were so close to the ultimate cable car technology that they formed the basis for later challenges to Hallidie's patents."

Not only was the idea of cable traction widespread and patented prior to San Francisco's first cable line, but also cables had been used to transport passengers in installations around the world. The first successful use of cable traction to move large numbers of people occurred in 1840 when the Blackwall Railway began operating in London—the very city where Hallidie's father manufactured wire rope. It operated by winding in and out a cable to which was attached the first car of a train. By the mid-1840s, all of the essentials of the cable car technology were available.

In addition, before Hallidie began building his cable line in San Francisco, Benjamin Brooks held a franchise for a cable haulage system there. He and his partners worked out details of their proposed system, but after they could not secure financing, they sold their franchise to none other than Andrew Hallidie.

AMERICA'S FIRST CABLE CARS

Charles Harvey designed and built the first cable car transit system to operate in the United States in 1867, four years before Hallidie built his first line in San Francisco. Harvey was no lightweight; he had built the Soo Canal joining Lake Superior and Lake Huron.

In 1866, Harvey patented a cable car system based on forks or claws on transit cars that could be lowered to engage discs or collars woven into a continuously moving steel cable. Stationary steam engines located under the sidewalk powered the cable. The following year, he built an experimental single-track elevated line using this technology in New York. In addition to being the first passenger cable car line in the United States, it is thought to be the world's first elevated transit line.

Intended to be the first leg of Harvey's West Side & Yonkers Patent Railway (WS&Y), this line operated along the east curb of Greenwich Street between Morris Street and

Running four miles along Greenwich Street in New York, the West Side & Yonkers Patent Railway was America's first cable car transit line. This is Car Number 1 at the 29th Street station. Note the Broadway omnibus (lower right). *New-York Historical Society.*

Battery Place at the southern tip of Manhattan. A test run on December 7, 1867, endorsed the concept and prompted investors to support the project. Revenue service began July 1, with cable cars traveling up to fifteen miles per hour. The WS&Y never reached its originally planned destination of Yonkers, New York, twenty-five miles north. Nevertheless, the cable line was extended north to Cortlandt Street and later to 32nd Street along Ninth Avenue, for a total length of four miles, with four stations.

Mechanical and financial problems plagued the company, which closed the line in 1870. New owners ran the line using small steam locomotives, but they failed after less than a year. The structure was torn down and replaced by a new elevated transit line.

Since the WS&Y ran in the nation's largest city, it is highly probable that its innovative cable car technology was widely noticed and discussed nationwide, especially in the trade press and among transit officials. Its demise must have discouraged the spread of cable car technology, whatever the design.

America's second cable car line was much more modest and ran for only six months in 1870 on an experimental basis. The three-block-long line involved a cable supported on arms above the track and powered by a stationary steam locomotive at each end of the line. Other than the fact that former Confederate General George Beauregard patented the technology, the most notable thing about this installation was its grip, which grabbed the cable simultaneously from above and below, similar to how the side grip would function years later.

SAN FRANCISCO'S CABLE CARS

This brings us back to Hallidie, who can be credited with pulling together many features of far-flung ideas and inventions to conceptualize, finance, build and operate the world's first long-lasting cable car transit system.

Andrew Smith was born in London in 1836 but later adopted the surname of his famous uncle, Sir Andrew Hallidie, who had been Queen Victoria's physician. As a boy, he was industrious. His Scottish father was an engineer who held patents for wire rope. Due to health problems, the father took his teenage son to California in 1852. When Andrew's father returned to London the following year, the young man stayed in California to prospect for gold. That did not pan out, but Andrew quickly proved to be a talented blacksmith, surveyor and builder, in particular by putting to use his expertise with wire rope that he had learned from his father. The young man moved to San Francisco and opened a wire rope manufacturing company. Hallidie built several suspension bridges, including a 220-foot-long bridge when he was only nineteen.

Soon, Andrew began to apply for patents of his own. One of these was in 1867 for the "Hallidie Ropeway or Tramway," a system for transporting ore and other materials in mines and through mountainous areas by means of an overhead, endlessly traveling cable. Two years later, he formulated a plan to adapt the endlessly traveling cable to streetcars, describing a system that used an underground cable and allowed railcars to grip the moving cable at will.

Securing financing for his idea, which became known as "Hallidie's Folly," proved difficult. After a year, he raised the money and hired engineer William Eppelsheimer. Together, they built a demonstration line on Clay Street from Kearny Street to Jones Street, a distance of only 2,800 feet that included a steep climb of 305 feet. On August 1, 1873, Hallidie tested his grip car early in the morning, perhaps so there would be no witnesses in case it failed.

On that day, the *Daily Bulletin* announced, "At five o'clock this morning the first car on the Clay St Railroad was sent down the hill and back again by means of the wire rope…No difficulty was experienced in stopping it at any point desired. The success of the experiment was greater than the projectors anticipated."

Despite the operational and commercial success that the Clay Street Hill Railroad soon enjoyed, Hallidie and others did not rush to build more cable lines. Many technological points needed to be worked out. Over the next nine years, only four additional cable lines were constructed in the United States, all of them in San Francisco. Each one was short and limited to eight miles per hour or less. By any reckoning—mileage, passengers, rolling stock, financial investment or public attention—this represented an inauspicious beginning for the cable car. Although a mechanical wonder, the cable car was viewed as an expensive but novel way to climb steep hills. That would change in the 1880s, once transit officials in Chicago took an interest.

CHAPTER 5

CABLE CARS
ON THE SOUTH SIDE

The progressive and well-managed Chicago City Railway operated the largest and most important cable car system ever in the United States, possibly the world. It played the pivotal role in propelling cable cars from a little-known solution for mastering San Francisco's hills into a nationwide urban transit industry.

CCR began as a horsecar company. In 1856, the Common (now City) Council granted a group of entrepreneurs the right to build a horse-drawn railway on unspecified streets. Only a short section of track was laid before financial difficulties caused by the Panic of 1857, a worldwide financial crisis, doomed the company.

On July 19, 1858, the Common Council granted another street railway franchise, this time to omnibus operator Franklin Parmelee. Mayor John Haines vetoed the measure on the grounds that if the city declined its option to purchase the railway at the end of twenty-five years, the company would get a perpetual franchise.

On August 16, the Common Council passed a third ordinance for horse-drawn streetcars. This franchise went, again, to Parmelee. The third time was to be a charm, leading, as it did, to Chicago's first street railway—but not right away. Within a few weeks, a judge placed an injunction on the horsecar line, ruling that the Common Council had overstepped its authority when it chartered Parmelee's company as a corporation. Under provisions of the state constitution, only the state legislature had the authority to charter a corporation. The judge also ruled that the city did not have the authority to franchise a railway or grant permission to use city streets for railway purposes.

During these legal wranglings and in the face of jeering onlookers who opposed railways on city streets, Parmelee's company began to construct a horsecar line on State Street near Randolph Street in November.

On February 14, 1859, the state (considered more powerful than the city, which it created) stepped in and resolved the legal issues. It incorporated Parmelee's CCR with the right to use streets on the South and West Sides for railway purposes, leaving the route up to the Common Council. The grant was limited to twenty-five years and gave the city the right to purchase the operation at the end of that period. At the same time, the legislature incorporated North Chicago City Railway and granted it the same rights and responsibilities for the North Side.

Thus, the stage was set for building street railways in Chicago. It is very telling that these early ordinances and legislative bills related to horsecars highlighted four contentious issues with which cable car companies, regulators and the public would wrestle years later: fares, franchise duration, regulatory jurisdiction and public ownership of transit.

ഐ൧൶

On April 25, 1859, CCR began operating Chicago's first street railway. The horsecars operated on State Street between Lake Street and 12th Street (now Roosevelt Road), a distance of about one mile. Although short and modest, the line launched the city's long and important rail transit history.

Over the years, the highly regarded CCR developed into Chicago's best street railway company and one of the most successful in the country. CCR attracted a parade of Chicago's top merchants and financiers as investors and directors. This started in 1864 with Samuel Nickerson, distiller, banker and organizer of the Union Stock Yards. Over the next few years, real estate magnate Silas Cobb, meatpacker Samuel Allerton and dry goods merchants Marshall Field and Levi Leiter joined the board.

Ironically, a steady turnover in ownership, starting with the sale of the company by Parmelee and his partners in 1864, helped keep the company's trustees open-minded

Previous pages: Chicago's first cable line ran on State Street and was wildly successful. Here, three-car CCR cable trains approach each other on State Street, each one towing an electric trolley car with its pole tied down. The photo was taken later in 1902 looking north from the Van Buren Street "L" station. Note how the horse-drawn wagon is traveling along the cable tracks for easier pulling and a smoother ride. *Chicago Transit Authority.*

Opposite page: CCR's State Street line had two destinations: 39th Street and 63rd Street. Its Cottage Grove Avenue line had three: 39th Street, Hyde Park (later renamed Jackson Park) and Oak Woods–71st Street. A train needed about one hour to reach downtown from any of these termini. *Roy G. Benedict | Publishers' Services.*

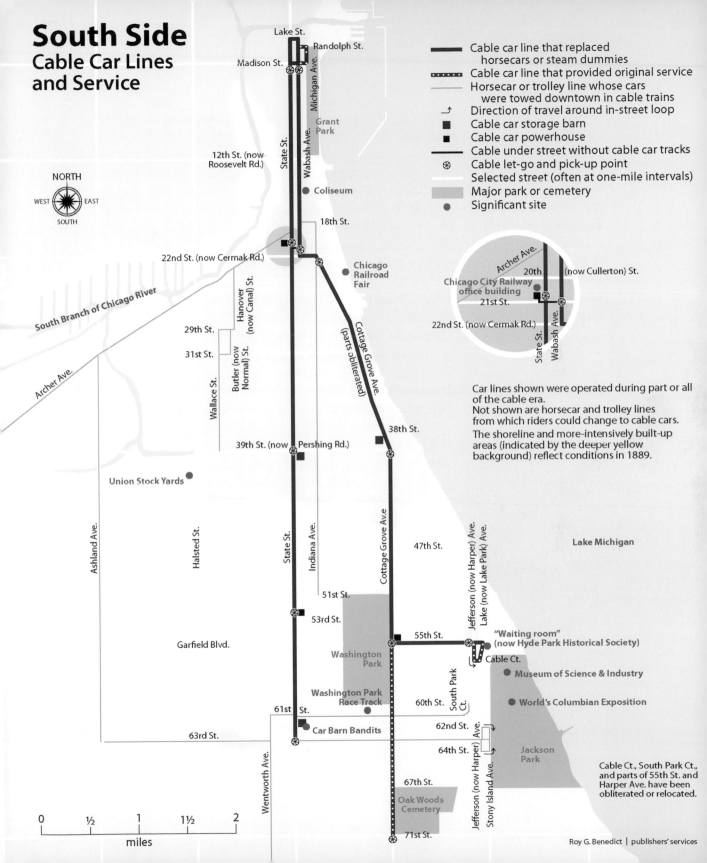

South Side
Cable Car Lines and Service

Legend:

━━━ Cable car line that replaced horsecars or steam dummies
▪▪▪ Cable car line that provided original service
─── Horsecar or trolley line whose cars were towed downtown in cable trains
↱ Direction of travel around in-street loop
■ Cable car storage barn
▪ Cable car powerhouse
━━━ Cable under street without cable car tracks
⊛ Cable let-go and pick-up point
─── Selected street (often at one-mile intervals)
▨ Major park or cemetery
● Significant site

NORTH
WEST EAST
SOUTH

Lake St.
Randolph St.
Madison St.
Michigan Ave.
Grant Park
Wabash Ave.
State St.
12th St. (now Roosevelt Rd.)
Coliseum
18th St.
22nd St. (now Cermak Rd.)
Chicago Railroad Fair
Cottage Grove Ave. (parts obliterated)
Hanover (now Canal) St.
29th St.
31st St.
Butler (now Normal) St.
Wallace St.
South Branch of Chicago River
Archer Ave.
38th St.
39th St. (now Pershing Rd.)
Union Stock Yards
Ashland Ave.
Halsted St.
State St.
Indiana Ave.
Cottage Grove Ave.
47th St.
Lake Michigan
51st St.
53rd St.
Garfield Blvd.
Washington Park
Washington Park Race Track
55th St.
Jefferson (now Harper) Ave.
Lake (now Lake Park) Ave.
"Waiting room" (now Hyde Park Historical Society)
Cable Ct.
Museum of Science & Industry
World's Columbian Exposition
South Park Ct.
60th St.
61st St.
63rd St.
Car Barn Bandits
62nd St.
64th St.
Jefferson (now Harper) Ave.
Stony Island Ave.
Jackson Park
Wentworth Ave.
67th St.
Oak Woods Cemetery
71st St.

Inset:
Archer Ave.
20th (now Cullerton) St.
Chicago City Railway office building
21st St.
22nd St. (now Cermak Rd.)
State St.
Wabash Ave.

Car lines shown were operated during part or all of the cable era. Not shown are horsecar and trolley lines from which riders could change to cable cars.

The shoreline and more-intensively built-up areas (indicated by the deeper yellow background) reflect conditions in 1889.

Cable Ct., South Park Ct., and parts of 55th St. and Harper Ave. have been obliterated or relocated.

0   ½   1   1½   2
miles

Roy G. Benedict | publishers' services

and its leaders innovative. By comparison, the principal street railways on the North and West Sides were run early on by cliques of conservative, stodgy investors and directors who resisted change and regarded horsecars as cash cows.

CCR's owners did not run the company directly or tinker with day-to-day operations. Instead, they turned over operations to professional managers. Of course, the investors expected a steady stream of dividends, but the company hired good managers and let them do their jobs. This open-mindedness contributed greatly to CCR's willingness years later to venture into cable traction.

Perhaps the best example of CCR's talented, professional managers who kept the street railway not only on track but also innovative was Charles Holmes. Regarded as one of the industry's most visionary leaders, Holmes would play the pivotal role in bringing cable cars to Chicago and assuring their success.

Born in Springfield, Vermont, Holmes moved to Belvidere, Illinois, to work as a teacher and farmer. In 1863, he became a coal merchant in Chicago. Ten years later, CCR hired him as superintendent, and by 1882, Holmes had risen to the rank of president, in which position he served until 1891.

Holmes became an ardent advocate of cable cars. Like his contemporary Daniel Burnham, Holmes made no small plans. In addition to the cable lines he would build on Wabash and Cottage Grove Avenues and State and 55th Streets, he had plans to install cable on Calumet, Wentworth and Indiana Avenues and Clark Street (all on the South Side).

With the help of many of CCR's well-heeled investors, Holmes developed National Railway. Through this traction syndicate, he purchased many street railways across the country, including two (St. Louis and Los Angeles) that later converted horsecar lines to cable.

Holmes was so convinced of the benefits of cable that he helped San Francisco's cable car innovators resolve outstanding patent issues nationwide. This led to the formation of the Cable Railway Company, a patent trust that would grow to encompass the patents of San Francisco's cable car innovators. Thus, Holmes helped disseminate cable car technology not only to Chicago but also around the country.

His career ended abruptly in 1891 when his street railway company in Los Angeles went bankrupt (due to a severe storm and exorbitant expenses related to the construction of its cable lines). This cost his Chicago backers nearly $2 million, so they pushed him out of CCR.

☥❦☦

CCR escaped the Great Chicago Fire of 1871 relatively unscathed because much of its infrastructure and equipment was south of the fire's path. This allowed the company to continue expanding aggressively, which helped build up the South Side. From the time of the fire until the end of the nineteenth century, much of Chicago's growth occurred southward, where development was not blocked by the Chicago River, as was the case on the North and West Sides.

It became increasingly apparent that steadfast but obsolete horsecars could not satisfy the transit needs of the dynamic, rapidly growing city. One of the many alternatives that showed promise was the cable car that had begun operating in San Francisco in 1873. Although many experts doubted that cable cars could function well in cold climates, CCR trustee Allerton was so impressed with the technology during a trip to San Francisco circa 1880 that he became a strong proponent. He encouraged CCR superintendent Holmes to go to San Francisco to see for himself. After a trip there in 1880, Holmes became even more enthusiastic than Allerton.

Upon his return, Holmes proposed converting CCR's most heavily traveled horsecar lines to cable, and his board quickly approved the plan, despite the enormous technological challenges and the huge financial investment involved. He also secured the blessing of Mayor Carter Harrison Sr., who predicted that cable cars would succeed in Chicago. The next step was to secure permission to "cablize" from the City Council. This was deemed necessary since CCR's original ordinance appeared to allow only animal-powered streetcars.

CCR requested permission on December 27, 1880, and the City Council granted it on January 17, 1881. This remarkably quick action without any objections or strings attached indicated that many aldermen might not have been paying attention over the holidays. Corruption, known as "boodle," was common in Chicago at this time. Aldermen expected bribes in exchange for favorable votes. Unscrupulous businessmen created shell railways to coerce established railways to buy out the potential competitors. And reformers stirred the pot, often with proposals that unintentionally made things worse, in part, by blocking rational planning and the integration of transit systems.

Some aldermen realized that they had let a potentially lucrative measure slip through their fingers when they approved CCR's request to cablize without extracting any boodle. Since the ordinance had already passed, they asked Mayor Harrison to veto the measure or at least delay signing it until they could "negotiate" with the company. The populist Harrison refused and signed the ordinance. Foiled on one front, the boodling aldermen found technical grounds for challenging CCR's right to operate cable cars along a section of its route. The challenge was quickly dropped, leading many to conclude that the company paid off the necessary parties.

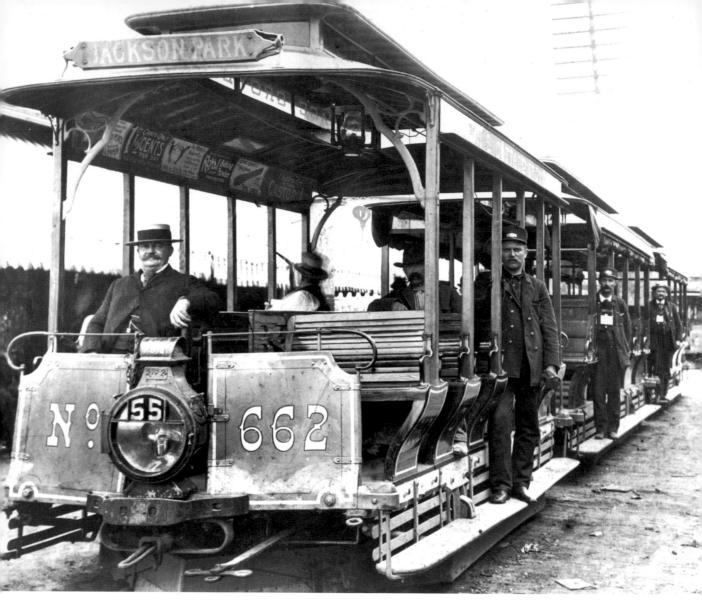

A Cottage Grove Avenue train heading for Jackson Park during or after the World's Columbian Exposition. Note one conductor per trailer and the running boards they are standing on. These could be folded up to avoid hitting oncoming trains. *Chicago Transit Authority.*

Besides paying illicit boodle, a transit company that wanted to build a cable line had to pay Cable Railway Company (the San Francisco patent trust) a legitimate licensing fee—or take the chance of getting sued for patent infringement. The going rate for use of the patents in the early 1880s was about $5,000 per mile.

With licenses in hand, Holmes would not have to reinvent the wheel. Nevertheless, he soon discovered that adapting the patented technology to the extensive needs of a big city and the punishing demands of cold weather was not easy. Holmes hired Asa Hovey as chief engineer for the conversion. Hovey had worked on the construction of two cable lines in San Francisco and was one of the chief patent holders. Despite such top bona fides, Hovey's job would be extremely difficult, in part because it was practically impossible to find engineers, contractors or laborers in Chicago with cable car construction experience.

Converting from horsecars to cable cars was not merely a matter of switching equipment. Existing horsecar tracks had to be replaced with an entirely new infrastructure that included an underground conduit through which the wire cable circulated. The conduit had to be strong to support the weight of street traffic. Furthermore, it had to be buried deeper than the conduit in San Francisco to keep the cable mechanisms below the frost line and to allow for the inevitable ice, snow and frozen manure to accumulate at the bottom without hindering the cable's movement.

The conversion began downtown on State Street in August 1881. Although they supported cable cars, merchants on State Street became irate over the street closure, detours and construction delays that piled up. They even marched on city hall.

CCR attributed construction delays to many causes. The cable car technology itself was novel and evolving. Many engineering, design and construction details needed to be perfected; others had to be adapted to local conditions. Innumerable underground water, gas and sewer pipes had to be replaced or moved at CCR's expense. And Chicago's notoriously muddy soil gave the builders endless headaches.

CCR's installation was by far the most ambitious cable car project undertaken up to that time, resulting in many unforeseen problems. New machinery had to be invented and built to handle the work. Shortages of supplies and labor wreaked havoc as well. Even though Chicago is flat, the soil was not solid enough to build a level cable line without extra work. Sloughs had to be filled in, consuming tons of stone. "Day after day saw load after load cast into these seemingly insatiable sink-holes, until the workmen declared an evil genie below removed the material as fast as it was thrown in," CCR reported.

A forty-two-inch-deep trough was dug, the yokes set in place every four feet and the concrete poured. The original rails were merely metal straps overlaid on wooden beams; later, they were replaced with a type of low-profile, grooved rail similar to what was later used for trolleys.

Drainpipes were installed along the conduit to carry water to the sewer. Steam pipes were laid at the bottom of the trough so a portable, horse-drawn boiler could introduce steam to melt any accumulated ice and snow. In addition to building the line, CCR had to pave and later maintain the center sixteen feet of State Street. It used six-inch-thick blocks of granite specially quarried for the job.

To build the first eight miles of track, CCR put 1,500 men and two hundred teams of horses to work for more than four months. They positioned four hundred tons of iron, forty-four thousand barrels of cement, 214,000 bricks, five hundred tons of steel rail and one hundred tons of timber into the conduit and track structure. The enormously expensive project cost $100,000 to $150,000 ($2.2 million to $3.3 million today) per double-track mile and nearly bankrupted CCR.

Finally, Chicago's first cable car line was ready. It ran on State Street from Madison Street to 21st Street, appropriately along the same route as Chicago's first horsecar line. On January 28, 1882, CCR inaugurated its cable car service with a festive ceremony. Revenue service opened to the public the next day. Trains ran 8½ miles an hour.

The grip cars were painted red, the same color as today's subway line under State Street.

On February 20, service was extended to 39th Street, then the southern limit of the city. It took a while to train gripmen, so for several weeks, CCR continued to operate horsecars alongside the cable cars.

≈∂∞∝

Although turntables to reverse the direction of a car were a common feature of cable car systems around the country, Chicago had only one (and it was built later on the North Side). Instead, CCR and Chicago's other transit companies built large rectangular cable car "loops" several blocks long running down the middle of four streets. Such single-track turning loops were less expensive to build, more efficient to operate and capable of handling much more traffic. They ran counterclockwise so that their track would not cross itself (given the fact that cable lines usually operated on the right side of the road). A cable line that crossed itself would have additional cable pick-up and let-go points, thereby increasing construction costs and operating difficulties.

The loops not only served the function of turning cars around but also extended each cable line a few blocks into new territory. Trains traveled around these loops picking up and dropping off passengers without lining up at a terminal point.

CCR built the first such loop from State and Madison Streets east to Wabash Avenue, north to Lake Street, west to State Street and south back to its starting point. It began operating on February 26, 1882, about a month after the State Street line opened.

This loop's cable was not issued from a powerhouse. Instead, it was an auxiliary cable connected to the main cable. Reduction gears cut its speed in half to about four miles an hour. This was the industry's first attempt with reduction gears, and it did not work well initially. Teams of horses had to be kept on hand to "make the jump" between the main cable and the auxiliary cable. After cable tension was adjusted and gripmen learned how to make the jump, riders "will see cable cars running up and down State Street in all their glory, without the aid of horse-power to do any switching at Madison Street," the *Chicago Tribune* said on February 24, 1882. Later, other cable systems around the country employed reduction gears to run an auxiliary cable from a main cable.

Eventually, Chicago's cable car companies built six downtown loops and a seventh in Hyde Park at the end of CCR's 55th Street cable line. The companies also built short oval loops inside car barns that were used to turn cars or make up trains. Some of these loops were not powered, in which case the cable cars had to be pushed or pulled by horses and/or employees.

ဢဢဢ

Many people have speculated about how the term "loop" became synonymous with downtown Chicago. The country's foremost cable car historian, George Hilton, attributed the term to the many cable car turnarounds known as "loops" that operated downtown. Many other historians, as well as the Commission on Chicago Landmarks, have stated the same thing. Recently, however, some historians have attributed the term to the elevated downtown track structure built in 1897 for the "L." But that rectangular "L" structure probably became known as a "loop" due to the prior practice of referring to downtown cable car turnarounds as "loops." Otherwise, that "L" structure (and possibly downtown Chicago) could have become known as the "ring," "circle," "rectangle," "turnaround" or something else.

Although no examples of the term "loop" in reference to the downtown area itself have been found relating to cable cars, it seems likely that the term "loop"—used so commonly during Chicago's cable car era—was later applied to the similar downtown "L" turnaround.

In any event, the term "loop" was used during the cable car era to refer not only to the cable car turnarounds but also to the cable car lines that had downtown turnarounds,

Following pages: In 1890, there were three cable car loops downtown. By 1894, that number had doubled. Meanwhile, the number of cable car tunnels under the Chicago River increased from two to three. *Roy G. Benedict | Publishers' Services.*

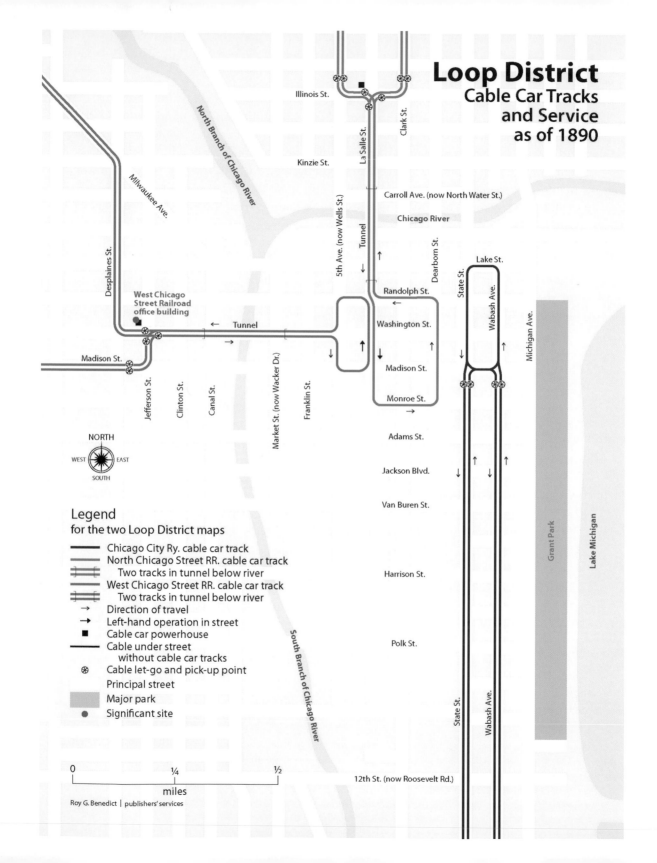

Loop District
Cable Car Tracks and Service as of 1890

Illinois St.

Kinzie St.

Carroll Ave. (now North Water St.)

Chicago River

La Salle St.

Clark St.

5th Ave. (now Wells St.)

Tunnel

Dearborn St.

Randolph St.

Washington St.

Madison St.

Monroe St.

Adams St.

Jackson Blvd.

Van Buren St.

Harrison St.

Polk St.

12th St. (now Roosevelt Rd.)

State St.

Wabash Ave.

Michigan Ave.

Lake St.

Grant Park

Lake Michigan

South Branch of Chicago River

North Branch of Chicago River

Milwaukee Ave.

Desplaines St.

West Chicago Street Railroad office building

Tunnel

Madison St.

Jefferson St.

Clinton St.

Canal St.

Market St. (now Wacker Dr.)

Franklin St.

NORTH
WEST EAST
SOUTH

Legend
for the two Loop District maps

Chicago City Ry. cable car track
North Chicago Street RR. cable car track
    Two tracks in tunnel below river
West Chicago Street RR. cable car track
    Two tracks in tunnel below river
→   Direction of travel
→   Left-hand operation in street
■   Cable car powerhouse
    Cable under street
    without cable car tracks
⊛   Cable let-go and pick-up point
    Principal street
    Major park
●   Significant site

0   ¼   ½
          miles

Roy G. Benedict | publishers' services

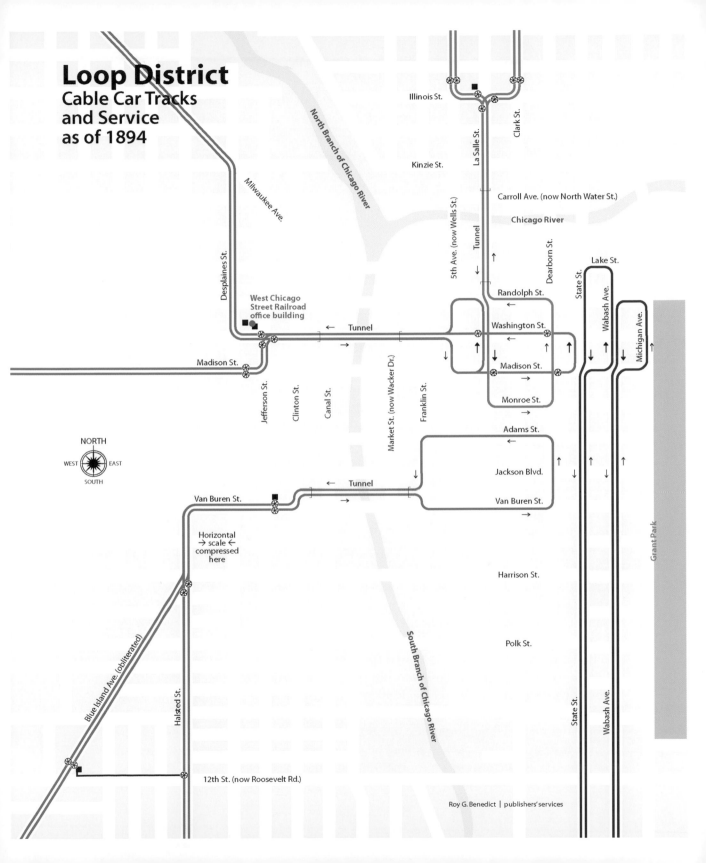

Loop District
Cable Car Tracks and Service as of 1894

Illinois St.

Clark St.

Kinzie St.

La Salle St.

Milwaukee Ave.

North Branch of Chicago River

Carroll Ave. (now North Water St.)

Chicago River

5th Ave. (now Wells St.)

Tunnel

Dearborn St.

Desplaines St.

West Chicago Street Railroad office building

Tunnel

Randolph St.

Washington St.

State St.

Lake St.

Wabash Ave.

Michigan Ave.

Madison St.

Jefferson St.

Clinton St.

Canal St.

Market St. (now Wacker Dr.)

Franklin St.

Madison St.

Monroe St.

Adams St.

Jackson Blvd.

Van Buren St.

Van Buren St.

Tunnel

Horizontal
→ scale ←
compressed
here

NORTH

WEST ⊕ EAST

SOUTH

Blue Island Ave. (obliterated)

Halsted St.

Harrison St.

South Branch of Chicago River

Polk St.

Grant Park

State St.

Wabash Ave.

12th St. (now Roosevelt Rd.)

Roy G. Benedict | publishers' services

as in "The [West Side] loop reaches the South Side through the Washington Street tunnel," from *Rand, McNally & Company's Bird's-eye Views and Guide to Chicago* published in 1893.

The bottom line: the common use of the term "loop" in Chicago originated in the cable car era—albeit as a reference to cable car track structures and cable car lines rather than to a geographic area. From there, it evolved and became a term that referred to downtown Chicago.

ᔕᔕ

While building the State Street line, CCR built a second cable line a block away on Wabash Avenue. It made sense to run a line close and parallel to the State Street line because traffic in and out of downtown was enormous. The new line went into service in January 1883 between Madison and 21st Streets. Soon afterward, the line was extended east on 22nd Street (now Cermak Road) and south on Cottage Grove Avenue to 39th Street.

The cable lines attracted new riders to transit. Serving Chicago's first upscale "Gold Coast" on Prairie Avenue, the much-ballyhooed cable cars were popular with the upper crust, even though they could afford a carriage or hackney. "Since the cable cars have begun to run on State Street the character of the passengers on that line has been completely revolutionized," Holmes told the *Omaha Daily Bee* in 1882, hyping his line. "All the fashionable people take this line now." This was the case, even though Chicago's cable cars never had a first-class section; rich and poor sat together.

At the north end of this line on Wabash and Cottage Grove Avenues (henceforth referred to as the Cottage Grove Avenue line), trains turned around using the same single-track downtown loop as the State Street line. Since this loop used two separate cables to carry the trains of the two separately operated lines, Hovey developed a double-jaw side grip. Besides allowing a railway to operate two cables through the same conduit, this grip was advantageous for handling curves. Its twenty-six-inch-long jaws to grab the cable were exceptionally strong, capable of pulling a ten-car train. This innovative grip was used around the country.

The need for a special grip was only one of the many challenges presented by the downtown loop. From the beginning, it was crowded. Northbound trains backed up south of Madison Street, sometimes as far as four blocks, waiting their turn to enter the loop. These bottlenecks on State Street and Wabash Avenue obstructed street traffic as well as cable traffic. The city compounded this problem for years by denying CCR permission for another downtown cable car loop.

A northbound State Street grip car at State and Adams Streets pulls a cable car trailer and an Archer Avenue trolley car with its pole tied down in 1905. *Chicago History Museum.*

In March 1892, with the Democratic Convention and 1893 World's Columbian Exposition looming, the city acquiesced on one of these points, granting CCR the right to build a second cable car loop. But where to put it? West Chicago Street Railroad (WCSR) held the franchise for streetcars on Michigan Avenue, while CCR held the franchise for streetcars on State Street. WCSR wanted rights to State Street in order to carry its passengers all the way to the myriad department stores and office buildings there, while CCR wanted rights to Michigan Avenue in order to build a second cable car loop to ease congestion on its first one.

Above: Shortly after cable cars débuted on State Street, CCR opened a parallel line one block east on Wabash Avenue. Here, a cable train heads south on Wabash Avenue near 9th Street in late 1905. Old St. Mary's Catholic Church is in the background. The lady in the street is probably heading for one of the smoke-free trailers. *Chicago Transit Authority.*

Opposite: Looking north on Cottage Grove Avenue at 39th Street in 1903. Horses were being used to make up a cable train outside CCR's car barn or because the cable was not operating at that time. Note the ad on the cable car for the Auto Show.

Long, complicated negotiations over trackage rights pitted Charles Holmes against Charles Tyson Yerkes, the aggressive broker turned transit tycoon who had by this time gained control of transit on the North and West Sides. Holmes was pushed out of his job, partly over this issue.

With Holmes out of the picture, the two companies finally agreed in 1892 to exchange their respective rights to Michigan Avenue and State Street. This allowed CCR to build its second downtown loop from Madison Street and Wabash Avenue, east to Michigan Avenue, north to Randolph Street, west to Wabash Avenue and south back to its starting point. Construction began in May and continued around the clock until it was completed the following month, just ten days before the convention opened.

The reduction gears at Madison Street and Wabash Avenue were removed as well as those at State and Madison Streets. Both loops were included as part of their respective line's main cable and operated up to $8\frac{1}{2}$ miles per hour. These changes relieved congestion considerably.

Operation on the Cottage Grove Avenue line originally suffered from another design flaw: two curves in close proximity on 22nd Street, where the line transferred between Wabash and Cottage Grove Avenues. Hovey originally addressed this hurdle with a low-speed cable just for the curves. CCR quickly realized, however, that it had overemphasized the difficulty of pulling cable cars around these two curves. In 1895, CCR removed the additional cable under 22nd Street and extended the Cottage Grove cable west to State Street and north to 21st Street. This did not eliminate the two curves, but it did eliminate one let-go and one pick-up point.

It was no surprise that CCR did not get everything right from the start, but astute company officials learned along the way. Soon South Side cable lines were operating

well, attracting riders, enhancing adjacent property values and enriching investors. Throughout most of the 1890s, CCR paid its stockholders an average of 12 percent in dividends—50 percent in 1893 due to the tremendous ridership generated by the World's Columbian Exposition.

☙❧

The quick success of cable cars on the South Side prompted CCR to keep building lines. In the spring of 1887, it extended its State Street cable line to 63rd Street in Englewood and added a powerhouse at 52nd Street. That November, CCR extended its Cottage Grove Avenue line south to 55th Street and east to Lake (now Lake Park) Avenue in Hyde Park, replacing a steam dummy line on 55th Street. This extension was operated from a new powerhouse at the northeast corner of 55th Street and Cottage Grove Avenue. CCR built a turning loop from 55th Street and Jefferson (now Harper) Avenue south to Cable Court (now obliterated), east to Lake (now Lake Park) Avenue, north to 55th Street and west back to its starting point.

Cable Court was more of a passageway than a street. Initially owned by Chicago City Railway, it was open to the public. Ironically, Cable Court was not named after cable cars but rather Ransom Cable, president of the Chicago Rock Island and Pacific Railroad from 1883 to 1898. (His magnificent former home still stands at 25 E. Erie Street.)

CCR constructed a small building along this loop at 5529 S. Lake (now Lake Park) Avenue in 1893, just in time for the world's fair. The historical record is not clear about the original purpose of this building, but it was called a "waiting room" and likely used as such by passengers and cable car crews.

Most of CCR's cable trains consisted of one grip car pulling two trailers. Initially, three trailers were allowed, with one train carrying what was then an astonishing 250 or more riders, but the city prohibited a third trailer in the 1890s on safety grounds.

Because large, proven traffic volumes were needed to recoup the huge expense of building a cable line, routes were primarily established through corridors with dense horsecar traffic. On the South Side, however, cable cars helped break new ground for the growing city that was gobbling up farms and prairies and annexing nearby suburbs at an unprecedented rate. The section of the Cottage Grove Avenue line south of 55th Street helped develop an area that had never been served by street railways.

When CCR extended its Cottage Grove Avenue line south to 67th Street in 1888, there were only four houses along the way. With so few residents, the cable cars were allowed to travel fourteen miles per hour, the top speed for Chicago's cable cars. Real

CCR built this "waiting room" at the end of its 55th Street cable car line in 1893 in anticipation of the heavy traffic that the World's Columbian Exposition would generate. It still stands at 5529 S. Lake Park Avenue and serves as the Hyde Park Historical Society's headquarters. *Photo by Jonathan Michael Johnson.*

estate speculators heavily subsidized the extension and later benefited as the area developed into an attractive residential district.

By 1887, CCR's cable cars were carrying up to 100,000 passengers a day, and the value of its stock had tripled. Its State Street line boasted the industry's heaviest traffic density. In 1888, CCR operated 263 trains simultaneously at rush hour. By 1892, that number had risen to 300.

That year, CCR extended its Cottage Grove Avenue line to the southern entrance of Oak Woods Cemetery at 71st Street. Counting the six blocks of the line's downtown loop, this line was almost ten miles long one way—the longest cable car line in the world ever. With so many extensions, the street railway estimated in 1890 that two-thirds of its income came from cable car operations, with the rest still coming from horsecars.

At its stub terminals at 63rd and 71st Streets (as well as at its intermediate 39th Street stop), CCR cable trains reversed direction using crossover tracks. The grip car, which could travel in either direction, simply switched tracks and picked up its trailer(s).

In addition to pulling cable car trailers, the grip cars often pulled horsecars and trolleys from connecting lines. This would delay service for the amount of time it took to attach or detach the trailer(s), which were sometimes located in the middle of the train. The conductor would stay with his car after it was transferred.

CCR upgraded its powerhouse at 55th Street and Cottage Grove Avenue with a pair of new engines in the 1890s. With thirty-eight-inch by seventy-two-inch cylinders, each engine was rated at 2,500 horsepower. They drove thirty-five-ton flywheels thirty-two feet in diameter. This pair of behemoths was capable of circulating twenty-two miles of cable.

80)03

CCR had hundreds of grip cars and maintained about four times as many trailers, which allowed the company to run two trailers per train, all the while maintaining two sets of trailers: open ones for the summer and closed ones for the winter. It built many of its own cable cars until 1893, when it could no longer keep up with the demand created by the World's Columbian Exposition.

Barns were needed to service and store cars, some overnight and others long term, out of season. In 1892, CCR built a massive state-of-the-art car barn at 39th and State Streets that housed 327 cars. The 206-foot-long structure included a full repair shop and washing facilities. It also provided a waiting room at its northwest corner, primarily for cable car passengers transferring for the Union Stock Yards, one mile west.

Elevators and central shunting tables on each of the three floors carried cars to their overnight berth or seasonal storage space on the upper floors. Since the first floor was fourteen inches above street level, cars entered the facility through momentum and exited through gravity. This eliminated the need for tow-boys, tow-horses and the "profanity, dirt, expense and superintendence required by these conveniences," as the company put it.

The 1892 car barn was a poorly timed investment because by then the end of the cable car era was impending. True, 66 percent of the company's revenue that year came from cable car operations. Plus, on October 21, dedication day at the world's fair, CCR collected 575,000 fares, mostly for cable car rides. That same year, however, the South Side "L" opened, cutting into CCR's cable traffic. More significantly, electric trolleys were beginning to play a role on the South Side. In early 1893, the

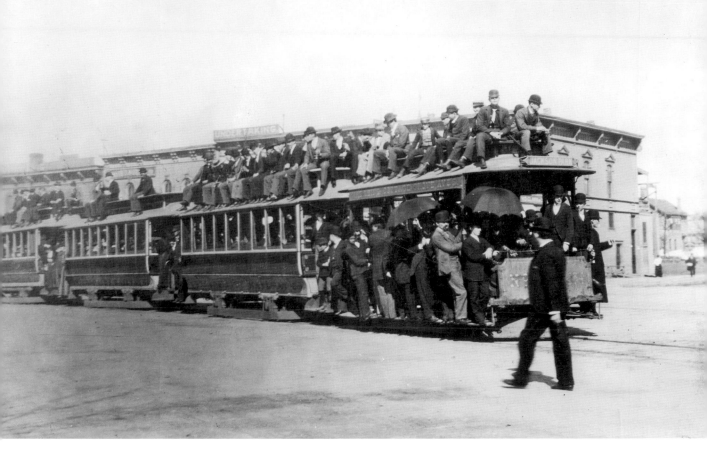

Cable car lines were well suited for heavy traffic, as demonstrated on Chicago Day at the World's Columbian Exposition of 1893 when a "virtually endless parade of cable trains, jammed almost beyond belief," carried 700,000 people. The fair featured several exhibits devoted to cable car technology, including one of the original Clay Street Hill Railroad cars from San Francisco's first line and a telescope Yerkes donated to the University of Chicago. Riding on the roof of cable cars was tolerated, especially on such busy days.

City Council allowed CCR to convert its horsecar lines on 47th, 61st and 63rd Streets to trolley to help the company cope with the huge number of riders anticipated for the fair.

The extra capacity paid off during the fair, especially on Chicago Day, October 9, 1893, when many Chicago businesses closed to encourage locals to attend the fair. That day, CCR set a record of 700,000 passengers, most of them on cable cars. The cars were so packed that throngs of cable car and trolley passengers rode on the roofs of cars, sometimes as many as 50 on top of one car. "The roofs were [covered] with people…and police were powerless to prevent them," the *Chicago Tribune* said on October 10. "Men and women sat in the windows, letting their feet hang out and dangle against the car side. The women who first so sat were greeted by cheers and laughter but they soon became so common as to excite merely smiles." When one car roof collapsed, "there would have been a panic but the people were packed in so closely that a panic could not make a living among them," said another newspaper.

CCR had about one thousand cars in service that day, allowing its president, George Wheeler, to boast, "No other city in the United States could transport within its limits in the same length of time so large a number of people as Chicago has done today."

CCR had come a long way since 1882 when the innovative horsecar company launched a nationwide expansion of cable cars. It had built seventeen and a half miles of double-track cable lines and three huge powerhouses that pulled thirteen separate cables. It had won support from Chicagoans and set a brisk pace for the entire cable car industry. Nevertheless, by 1893, the industry had begun its unalterable decline.

CHAPTER 6

SOUTH SIDE
CAR BARN BANDITS

Early in the history of cable cars, some wealthy businessmen who were approached about investing in the technology declined to invest because they did not think the huge costs of financing, constructing, operating and maintaining cable lines could be recouped one nickel at a time. But those nickels added up—so much so that transit companies in Chicago were encouraged to count and deposit their receipts as quickly as possible to avoid creating a local shortage of coinage.

All those nickels attracted the attention of thieves as well. That's where the money was, to paraphrase renowned bank robber Willie Sutton. Throughout the 1880s and 1890s, there were occasional robberies of cable car receipts in Chicago, but one theft stands out above the others. That deadly heist of $2,250 in 1903 was the work of the Car Barn Bandits, "without a doubt the most reckless and daring quartet of youthful desperadoes that ever operated in Chicago or vicinity," according to Police Superintendent Francis O'Neill (a noted musicologist who happens to be the namesake of Chief O'Neill's Pub and Restaurant on Chicago's North Side).

The members of the gang that became known as the Car Barn Bandits were Chicago's first celebrity criminals, and their crimes were tracked in newspapers across the country. They inflicted nothing less than a "reign of terror" on Chicago from July to November 1903, killing eight people, including two police detectives, and wounding five more. They brandished relatively new weapons—automatic pistols—and killed with a blatant disregard for life that portended the violence and gang warfare of the 1920s for which Chicago would become so well known.

Like Al Capone and his gangsters, these thugs were young. Their swaggering ringleader, Harvey Van Dine, was twenty-one years old, as was Peter Niedermeyer. Gustave Marx was twenty-two, and their frequent sidekick, Emil Roeski, was only

The Car Barn Bandits foreshadowed Chicago's criminal activity of the 1920s, including that of Al Capone's gangsters, who used the Lexington Hotel (seen here) on Michigan Avenue as their headquarters. After robbing CCR's car barn at 61st and State Streets, the Car Barn Bandits reportedly took this cable car line downtown. This train is heading west on 22nd Street. *Chicago History Museum.*

nineteen. Accounts of their childhood vary, but their criminal career apparently began when, as boys, they joined the Monticello Pleasure and Athletic Club, a group of youthful ruffians who hung out on Monticello Avenue near the North Branch of the Chicago River. In 1901, they impressed their fellow thugs by stealing some lead pipes and brass fittings and selling them for a tidy sum.

In the summer of 1903, these criminals purchased the automatic pistols. Working in a group of two or three, they became more brazen. In July, they robbed the Clybourn Junction station of the Chicago & North Western Railway, shooting an employee in the process. The same month, they held up three saloons, killing a boy and shooting one of the owners. In August, they killed two men while holding up a saloon. "We got eight dollars out of that haul," Van Dine said later. "We killed two men—four dollars a piece."

As the summer of 1903 wore on, the gang became increasingly cavalier about killing, but their murderous rampage had netted only about $200. They decided to go after bigger loot: Chicago City Railway's cable car barn at 61st and State Streets. Built in 1887, this massive, three-story brick building could store 330 cars. By 1903, CCR employed 212 conductors and 203 gripmen, motormen and horsecar drivers at this location.

At 3:00 a.m. on August 30, three clerks were tallying the previous day's receipts when Niedermeyer, Marx and Van Dine approached the facility. The bandits walked in at gunpoint. When the employees resisted, a volley of bullets killed clerk Frank Stewart and motorman James B. Johnson. After using a sledgehammer to break into an adjacent office, the bandits found enough money to satisfy themselves. They ran east to Jackson Park, the still abandoned site of the World's Columbian Exposition of 1893. When the sun rose, they hid in a clump of bushes and divided up the money. Then they rode downtown, most likely on a cable car owned by the very company they had just robbed.

Learning from a witness of the rapidity with which the shots were fired, the police realized that the bandits were armed with "a new make of gun known as the automatic," according to the police report. "This information was given to every officer on the force, and a man-hunt was taken up for the most desperate band of criminals that ever infested Chicago."

The young, careless bandits spent their money ostentatiously, which generated suspicion since they did not work or come from wealthy families. In the middle of November, the police heard that Marx was spending money recklessly and showing off an automatic revolver. Two officers found him in the saloon at Robey Street (now Damen Avenue) and Addison Street. When the officers tried to apprehend him, Marx pulled out his automatic pistol and killed one of them. The other officer shot and disarmed Marx.

Marx was taken into custody and confessed to several crimes, including the car barn robbery. He also gave the names of his fellow bandits. The police later bragged that the confession was secured by a "rigid examination" and even named the heavy-handed interrogator: Assistant Chief Herman F. Schuettler.

"There are carping critics of this department who maintain that to 'sweat' or persistently interrogate a prisoner is barbarous and that such a practice should be abolished," wrote Superintendent O'Neill in his 1903 report to the City Council. "All

Police pose at an abandoned cellar in the Indiana Dunes where the Car Barn Bandits had been found hiding. *Chicago History Museum.*

I care to say in reply is that if the 'stomach pump,' as it is sometimes called, had not been applied to Marx he never would have confessed to complicity in the raid on the car barn; neither would he have 'squealed' on his accomplices in that and several other crimes."

Photographs of the three bandits remaining at large were circulated and printed in local newspapers. The criminals fled to northwest Indiana. When they stopped at a grocery on Thanksgiving Day, someone recognized them from the newspaper photographs and contacted the Chicago police. The ensuing chase trapped the bandits in an abandoned cellar in the Indiana Dunes. When police demanded their surrender, the youths came out shooting—killing one officer and wounding another. With guns blazing, they escaped into the countryside.

The handsome, five-foot, nine-inch-tall Yerkes was fit and vigorous. Men found him charismatic; women found him charming, even irresistible. Yerkes's professional and social standing rose meteorically. This happy state was not to last, however, and Chicago was to play a major role in Yerkes's downfall.

RUIN

Yerkes began to trade city bonds and became an agent of the city treasurer. As such, he did much to increase Philadelphia's credit and financial standing. For this he was well rewarded and increasingly trusted.

At this time, vague financial controls allowed investors and accountants, bankers and brokers to engage in financial chicanery, frequently dipping into public funds for personal gain or to cover their debts. Yerkes "manipulated the flow of this river of public money, frequently diverting a portion of the stream into his pockets" and those of friends and colleagues, according to John Franch in *Robber Baron*.

In the summer of 1871, Yerkes took a huge gamble, betting that a favorable court ruling concerning the Pennsylvania Railroad would cause the value of that stock to increase. He purchased nearly $5 million of stock in Pennsylvania Railroad and other railroads.

On October 8, only days before Yerkes's anticipated favorable ruling and subsequent windfall, a fire broke out in Chicago. As a result, markets fell nationwide. Railroad stocks were hit especially hard. As the Great Chicago Fire raged, destroying much of the city, the national markets panicked and crashed.

Yerkes had borrowed heavily to leverage his railroad stock purchases, and his creditors demanded their money. When it became clear that Yerkes could not pay his creditors or borrow additional money to cover his losses, he was financially ruined. He owed more than $1 million with assets in the neighborhood of $250,000.

To make matters worse, Yerkes had put public funds at risk. He had done so often before, but this time he would not get away with it. He had used $300,000 of city funds in his colossal railroad speculation and secured an additional $33,000 from the city by asking to be reimbursed for city bonds that he had not, in fact, purchased. When he could not repay the city, he was charged with embezzlement and larceny. He went from rising star to scoundrel.

Throughout the ensuing trial, Yerkes was confident he would get off, claiming that other financiers did similar things and that he was being scapegoated. He maintained

Once Yerkes got control of transit on the North Side, he acted quickly to introduce cable service. This crowded Wells Street NCSR cable train sits at the Limits car barn in 1892. Open cars had cloth curtains (seen here) that could be lowered in the case of rain. Gripman Robt. Pattison stands on the grip car in the front. *Chicago Transit Authority.*

that he would have been able to pay all of his debts if only the Great Chicago Fire had not caused the markets to crash.

A jury found Yerkes guilty, and he was sentenced to two years and nine months in prison. A few days later, he was declared bankrupt; shortly afterward, he was imprisoned. The thirty-four-year-old former millionaire took up residence as inmate 7126 in a seven- by seventeen-foot cell at Philadelphia's notorious Eastern State Penitentiary.

From that experience, Yerkes developed contempt for the legal system and the press. He maintained that he had been made an example to appease an irate public and to hide broad, systemic financial trickery. Before this time, he had aspired to join the upper crust of society; afterward, he disdained "respectable" business and political leaders. His new thick skin would serve him well years later in Chicago.

Yerkes smoldered in prison for a few months but hoped for an early release. An attempt to blackmail influential politicians and other schemes failed to rescue him. Ultimately, Yerkes managed to get out of prison after serving seven months by inserting himself into upcoming state and national elections.

Pennsylvania Attorney General John Hartranft had his sights set on becoming governor of Pennsylvania. Hartranft, however, had a skeleton in his closet that threatened his chances of winning. A former client of Yerkes, he had engaged in illegal speculation with public funds, according to an affidavit that Yerkes had filed years earlier. The affidavit was leaked to the press, and the revealing document seemed to doom Hartranft's chances of being elected governor.

The importance of Hartranft's predicament escalated when leaders of the national Republican Party concluded that if Hartranft lost, President Ulysses S. Grant would lose Pennsylvania, whose twenty-nine electoral votes were considered key to Grant winning a second term. The situation was so perilous that Grant reviewed the matter.

When it became clear that Yerkes was willing to deny the authenticity of his affidavit incriminating Hartranft in

After receiving much negative press, Yerkes published this promotional booklet portraying North Side cable operations in a favorable light. The cover depicts the LaSalle Street tunnel that he converted to cable car service. *Chicago History Museum.*

exchange for being pardoned, Grant ordered John White Geary, Pennsylvania's soon-to-retire Republican governor, to pardon Yerkes. Within days, Yerkes was freed and renounced his affidavit against Hartranft, making front-page news. Shortly thereafter, Hartranft was elected governor of the Quaker State, and Grant carried the state and was reelected president.

REBIRTH

After being released from prison, Yerkes floundered a while. He tried to mine gold in New Hampshire. When that failed, he returned to finance. Yerkes paid back some of his debts and, in 1873, persuaded his creditors to release him from bankruptcy. From there, he rebuilt his brokerage business.

Yerkes had been introduced to street railways in the early 1860s by Anthony Drexel, a member of the prestigious banking family who induced him to purchase stock in a Philadelphia street railway. The investment turned out to be profitable. True to form, Yerkes came to own half of that company's stock and took the opportunity to master the street railway business.

Yerkes lost all of his shares in that street railway when he went bankrupt in 1871, but after rebounding in the mid-1870s he invested heavily in streetcar companies. He purchased shares in the Continental Passenger Railway, became a director and soon became the largest shareholder in that company. He bought at $15 a share and eventually sold at nearly $100 a share.

At Continental, Yerkes worked with Philadelphia transit tycoon, politico and wheeler-dealer William Kemble. Yerkes would learn an enormous amount about finance, politics and street railways—as well as bribery, stock manipulation and influence peddling—from this traction kingpin. Among other things, he mastered "addition, subtraction and silence," referring to a reticence to discuss his business affairs. He would put many of these lessons to good use years later in Chicago.

Kemble had formed Continental to rival the established Union Passenger Railway. After years of machinations—and some jail time of his own—Kemble bought Union. As a major Continental stockholder, Yerkes complained that he had been left out of important decisions regarding that deal. This led to a falling out with Kemble. Nevertheless, Yerkes would later turn to Kemble and two of his lieutenants, Peter Widener and William Elkins, to finance traction deals.

CHICAGO BECKONS

By 1880, Yerkes had decided to leave Philadelphia. Why is not certain, but the falling out with Kemble was a factor. Also, as an ex-con, he and his wife were socially ostracized. Perhaps most importantly, he wanted to leave his wife. The forty-three-year-old Yerkes had fallen for the strikingly beautiful twenty-two-year-old Mary Adelaide Moore.

That year, Yerkes visited Chicago for the first time. By all accounts, he was impressed with the dynamic city, where everyone seemed engaged in the pursuit of money. In 1881, he went to Fargo in the Dakota Territory, where divorces were relatively easy to obtain. He made some money in real estate, but Fargo was too small for his ambitions. Chicago, then the nation's second-largest financial center and possibly the most freewheeling city in the country, drew him like a moth to flame. In November 1881, Yerkes and his new wife moved there and purchased a home in a fashionable district at 1726 (now S.) Michigan Avenue.

Charles opened a brokerage, joined the Chicago Board of Trade and began trading grain and commodities. The following year, he was elected to the prestigious Union League Club. After learning of his prison time, divorce and remarriage to a woman half his age, however, the club barred him. This foreshadowed the difficulties the Yerkeses would have over the next two decades trying to break into Chicago's upper crust. In 1884, Charles and Mary moved to a larger house at 3201 (now S.) Michigan Avenue, but they were never accepted by Chicago's "sifted few."

Although snubbed socially, Charles fit in with the hard-driving, competitive business community and interacted continuously with Chicago's business and industrial leaders. Most of that story will be recounted in the chapters of this book devoted to the West Side and North Side street railways. Here we pick up the story in the early 1890s after Yerkes had already acquired those two companies. Having introduced cable cars to the West and North Sides, Yerkes was now known as Chicago's Cable Car Czar. He controlled about 250 miles of streetcars, 47 miles of which were cable. At the same time, he was dabbling in "L" lines and other forms of traction.

Yerkes was driven and devious, a financial wizard who derived enormous profits from managing and manipulating stocks, bonds and other people's money. He made even more money by creating complex corporate structures and business relationships that were so layered and obtuse that they defied scrutiny.

He also made money through real estate development. Streetcar lines, real or proposed, were often used to develop tracts of farms and fields into residential areas. At one point, Yerkes teamed up with real estate developer Samuel Gross, who built a huge number of affordable homes for working-class Chicagoans. Yerkes would buy land, run a streetcar line through it, hire Gross to build the streets, sewers and homes and watch the real estate appreciate.

Many Chicago businessmen distrusted him, and a growing number of them refused to deal with him. Some of his enemies included Marshall Field, with whom he had locked horns regarding investments; Levi Leiter, who fought Yerkes over the location of the Loop "L"; Ferdinand Peck, who had tried to gain control of the North Chicago City Railway but lost out to Yerkes; Melville Stone, a *Chicago Daily News* publisher

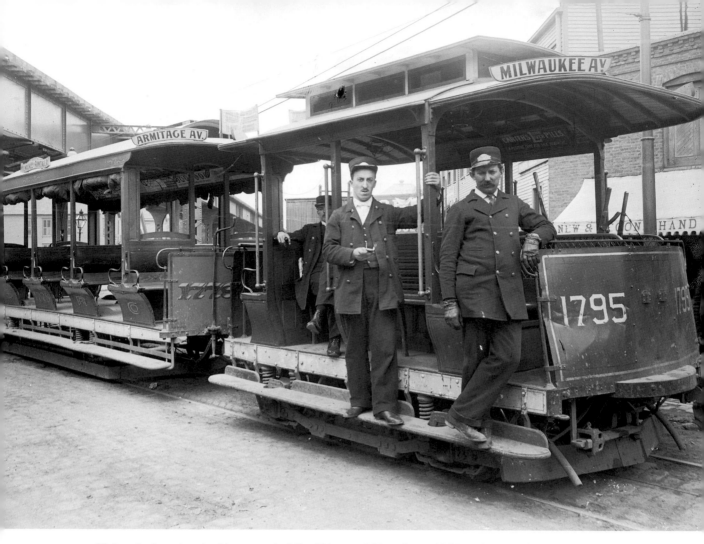

Yerkes also introduced cable cars to the West Side as quickly as he could. Near the start of a trip downtown, crew members pose with their eastbound Milwaukee Avenue cable train on Armitage Avenue underneath the shiny new Logan Square "L" structure. *Chicago History Museum.*

whom Yerkes had threatened to kill; and Joseph Medill, a reformer, Chicago mayor and *Chicago Tribune* publisher.

Usually a transit proponent, Yerkes was not above blocking a transit line to stymie a competitor. Such was the case in 1888 when he opposed a proposed horsecar line on a new bridge over the South Branch of the Chicago River at Jackson Street (now Boulevard)—even though he had previously proposed running his own streetcars on that very bridge. Author and intrepid tour guide David Clark has revealed an odd alliance between Yerkes and residents of Jackson Street who were opposed to transit on their street.

Yerkes wanted to keep his street railway competitors on the West Side from gaining a new inroad into the business district, Clark wrote in the Fall 2009 *Route 66 Magazine*. "To keep street rail off the Jackson Street bridge, a petition was circulated to property owners along the thoroughfare calling for Jackson Street to be designated as a park boulevard, off limits to commercial teaming wagons and rail franchises. This would come at a price, since boulevard conversion would be paid for by the property owners through a special property tax assessment."

Yerkes overcame the objections of recalcitrant property owners and persuaded them to support the petition by agreeing to pay most of the conversion cost himself. The boulevard ordinance passed in 1896, and the competitor's horsecar line was not built. (Years later, the lack of streetcars on Jackson Boulevard made it attractive to automobiles and led to the routing of Route 66 along that street, Clark concluded.)

WORLD'S COLUMBIAN EXPOSITION

Despite having many enemies, Yerkes was one of Chicago's richest and most influential people. As such, he was drawn to planning and financing the World's Columbian Exposition. By 1893, however, Chicago's business leaders regarded him as dishonest and too powerful.

When his rivals sought to deny him a seat on the fair's board, Yerkes pledged to buy $150,000 in fair stock, more than anyone else. This guaranteed him a seat on the board. Yerkes did not get his money's worth, however. The board was stacked with South Siders, which assured that the fair would be located in that part of town, even though 60 percent of the population lived on the West Side, where the Cable Car Czar controlled transit. Try as he did, Yerkes could not derail the decision to locate the fair on the South Side, where he had no transit holdings—but he made more enemies in the process.

Although South Side transit concerns benefited the most from the fair, all transit systems enjoyed a spike in ridership. In 1893, Yerkes's North Chicago Street Railroad carried ten million more riders than the previous year, for a total of sixty million riders. Profits rose $400,000.

Many exhibits at the fair featured cable cars and related items, including a telescope that Yerkes gave the University of Chicago and Clay Street Hill Railroad's grip car Number 8, one of the original cars from San Francisco's first line. (This car is on display at the Cable Car Museum in San Francisco, the only such remaining car.)

After the fair, Yerkes teamed up with George Washington Ferris to restore what had been the iconic symbol of the fair. In 1895, they reassembled the giant Ferris wheel in Ferris Wheel Park at Clark Street and Sherman (now Drummond) Place, across the street from the Limits car barn at the end of Yerkes's Clark Street cable line. This did not generate enough nickel fares on cable cars or half-dollar admissions on the wheel to justify expenses, so the wheel was dismantled in 1903 and sent to St. Louis for the Louisiana Purchase Exposition of 1904.

Meet the Press

Yerkes owed much of his bad reputation to the thrashings he regularly endured from Chicago's newspapers, many of which were sensational and biased. To sell newspapers, the press needed villains. Yerkes came ready-made!

"The press of Chicago has no favorable regard or respect for a fellow who uses Chicago for a milch cow…who grabs franchises in Chicago and uses their excessive profits to erect a palace in New York crammed with pictures, bric-a-brac and luxuries of the most costly kind," seethed *Chicago Tribune* editor Joseph Medill.

The newspapers held Yerkes responsible for rickety horsecars and crowded cable cars. Later, they blamed him for "dangerous" trolley cars and their exposed electrical wires. "Death in the Air" rang out one headline. Yerkes could not win. He tried to tell his side of the story by purchasing the *Inter Ocean* in 1895, but that did not make much difference. The "Transit Titan" became increasingly unpopular with the public.

Yerkes tried to burnish his image through public largess. In 1888, he purchased a lion for the Lincoln Park Zoo. Two years later, he donated an electric fountain to Lincoln Park at the cost of $50,000 ($1.2 million today). The spectacular fountain contained more than two hundred water jets and shot water one hundred feet in the air. "At each change of color the crowds of spectators utter fresh exclamations of pleasure," said *Electrical Engineer*. "Twice a week in the summer, 20,000 to 80,000 spectators gather to see the brilliant show," said *Harper's Weekly*.

But such beneficence did not win over many people. Religious reformer William Stead wrote in his 1894 book *If Christ Came to Chicago*, "Mr. Yerkes, having acquired so many millions from Chicago, graciously deigns, now and then, of his munificence to throw a sop or two to the public." Such work "might be regarded as a shrewd business speculation, for the greater the attraction in Lincoln Park the more dense was the packing in Mr. Yerkes' cars."

The gift of an observatory to the University of Chicago, however, could not have been motivated by a desire to fill streetcars because it was located on the shore of Lake Geneva in Williams Bay, Wisconsin. Yerkes's transit lines did not reach quite that far.

When William Rainey Harper, president of the newly created University of Chicago, and astronomy professor George Ellery Hale approached Yerkes in 1892 about funding a telescope, they appealed to the Cable Car Czar's ego. Why not build a huge telescope and name it after him? Genuinely interested in astronomy since boyhood—and in need of some good public relations—Yerkes accepted the challenge. Uncharacteristically, he was cornered into funding not just one telescope but an entire observatory with five telescopes, one of which remains the world's largest refracting telescope.

Designed by Henry Ives Cobb, the observatory was dedicated in 1897. Yerkes contributed more than $285,500 ($7.4 million today) to the cause, far more than he initially intended. Still, even that was not enough to buy him a favorable mention in some quarters. "The astronomical beneficence of Mr. Yerkes does not excuse his street railway shortcomings any more than the educational liberality of Mr. Rockefeller justifies the methods of Standard Oil," said the *Chicago Times*. "It begins to look as if President Harper's success as a money raiser was due to his having shrewdly represented the Chicago University to diverse men of wealth as a sort of conscience fund."

The cover of reformer William Stead's 1894 book, *What If Christ Came to Chicago*, that indicted Chicago's corruption and vice. It depicts Yerkes scooping up money and clutching a cable car at Jesus' feet. *Chicago Public Library, Special Collections and Preservation Division.*

Due to Stead's prodding, the Civic Federation was formed to wipe out "all the elements of evil" in Chicago. It targeted the Goliath of Graft, awakened the public and galvanized strong anti-Yerkes sentiments that would hound "the street railway despot of Chicago," as Stead called him, out of town.

Building Transit…and Enemies

As soon as he gained control of the North Side street railways, Yerkes embraced cable car technology. Nonetheless, once he decided that electric traction was feasible and more profitable than other transit systems, he pursued it with force and vigor, despite the money he had already invested in cable cars. In fact, Yerkes did more to electrify Chicago's transit network than any other person. He was always innovative, quick to experiment with new ideas and willing to throw money into those that worked.

Yerkes converted his steam-powered Lake Street "L" to electric power and planned the Northwestern "L" as an electric line from the beginning. Regarding surface lines, between 1894 and 1899, Yerkes converted more than one hundred miles of Chicago's horsecar trackage to electric trolley, leapfrogging cable car technology. This dramatically improved transit and transformed Chicago.

At the same time, Yerkes turned his attention to the suburban electric lines that ringed Chicago. Between 1894 and 1897, he acquired eight such lines north and west of the city, some of which were not yet operational. These suburban lines, which added more than fifty miles to Yerkes's streetcar empire, not only fed customers into his Chicago streetcar lines but also increased the city's reach into surrounding areas, dramatically extending the size and scope of the booming metropolis.

Yerkes, who according to the *Chicago Tribune* had "some strange and wondrous methods of doing business," kept these suburban companies corporately distinct from each other and from his Chicago streetcar companies, even though he often talked about his vision of a widespread, integrated and "harmonious" transit system. Critics called this approach an excuse to charge multiple fares. For his part, Yerkes insisted that a nickel could carry a passenger only so far before the company would lose money on that ride.

A true transit visionary, Yerkes also built a long-sought, oft-discussed downtown Loop "L" to connect the previously built "L" lines, all of which had been kept out of the city center due to competitive pressure, fear of steam locomotives operating overhead and concerns about the impact of an elevated structure on property values along its route. Yerkes battled business owners along all four sides of the Loop "L" before finally prevailing.

In 1895, Yerkes hopped aboard the nationwide bicycle boom and became a "bicycle crank," as he put it. "I formerly spent hours daily in such exercises as are found in the gymnasium, but I have given all that up. The wheel is the thing and I am positive of it." Fashionably clad in knickerbockers and a tight-fitting sweater that showcased his still-athletic form, Yerkes pedaled every day on the South Side boulevards.

WCSR had to negotiate hard for the rights to move the eastern side of its original cable car loop from LaSalle Street to State Street, thereby gaining access to that "Great Street's" many department stores, including Siegel, Cooper's & Company's Big Store at Congress Street (now Parkway) in the Second Leiter Building. A CCR cable train heads north on State Street. Note the Auditorium Building's tower in the background. *Chicago History Museum.*

Pulling Back

Within ten years of his arrival, Yerkes was disillusioned with Chicago. He opened an office on New York's Wall Street and, in 1891, purchased a large piece of land on Fifth Avenue overlooking Central Park on "Millionaires' Row." Two years later, he began to build a majestic four-story mansion there that would end up costing more than $1.5 million ($36 million today). He furnished it opulently and filled it with fine art. Further evidence that he intended to leave Chicago was his purchase of a mausoleum in Brooklyn for him and his wife. "I am in Chicago to make money," he said, "and if it were not for what I expect to make out of it I would take the first train to New York and never set eyes on the beastly place again."

At the same time, Yerkes and his second wife, Mary, were drifting apart. Rumors abounded that he had numerous mistresses. Some of them were supposedly the wives of leading Chicago businessmen.

In 1896, Yerkes came to the brink of financial ruin twice but held off his creditors through bluff and intimidation, as well as financial wizardry and stock manipulation. Doing business in Chicago was becoming more difficult as reformers, including the Municipal Voters' League organized in 1896, ousted one boodling alderman after another, thereby reducing Yerkes's influence on the City Council.

In 1899, Yerkes took more steps to consolidate his transit holdings. Again, he created a confusing combination of overlapping companies that shared power and trackage and were tied together legally and financially. In February, he incorporated the Chicago Consolidated Traction, which purchased eight small transit companies north and west of the city. In May, he incorporated Chicago Union Traction to buy out his North and West Side transit companies. Union Traction issued $12 million in new stock, $9 million of which was used to pay Yerkes when WCSR and NCSR were rolled into Union Traction.

Just prior to this deal, Yerkes had given Consolidated Traction the right to run its trains downtown on WCSR and NCSR tracks. This devious move was designed to force Union Traction to purchase Consolidated Traction. It worked, and Yerkes pocketed another $4 million. By December 1899, Union Traction controlled all these entities, including forty-nine miles of cable car operations.

But Yerkes did not stop there. He wanted to merge Union Traction with his Lake Street, Northwestern and Loop elevated lines. Opposition from politicians, competitors, reformers, the public and the press prevented this. They feared the Transit Titan's power and resented his growing and conspicuous wealth.

After losing a long-fought battle over street railway franchises, Yerkes was done with the city he had commandeered for more than a decade. In 1899, he sold his transit lines to his on-again, off-again Philadelphia partners and former business enemies Field and Leiter, among others. Chicago's Cable Car Czar moved to his well-furnished New York mansion, despite lingering complications over the construction of his Northwestern "L" and consolidation of his street railways. The energetic sixty-two-year-old was wealthy enough to relax in regal retirement in his mansion, which the *New York Times* described as "one of the finest and most-talked-of Fifth Avenue residences."

The sign on the front of this grip car says, "Take this car to Ferris Wheel Park," which NCSR had built in 1895 at the end of its Clark Street cable line near Sherman (now Drummond) Place. *James J. Buckley Collection.*

Before he had the chance to settle in, however, he became intrigued by an offer from would-be partners to finance and build an electric subway in London. Despite being the largest city in the world and roughly three times the size of Chicago, London was burdened with archaic transit facilities. Having banned streetcars from the city center, London was overly dependent on horse-drawn taxis and omnibuses. The city did have four subway lines, but only one of them was successful.

After visiting London to survey the project, Yerkes decided to take the plunge. True to form, he did not hold back. Soon he was proposing to electrify one of the existing subways and build three new lines, for a total network of twenty-four miles of underground railways. He sought no less than $25 million ($647 million today) to finance this monumental endeavor, a sum that grew over time. As with his other endeavors, the finances for this deal were extremely complex and involved novel financial instruments. Some called this creative genius; others called it a house of cards.

The plot thickened when a scheme supported by J.P. Morgan was proposed that would have built subways in direct competition with Yerkes's budding network. When Parliament approved Morgan's proposal, it included an "all or nothing" clause. Yerkes

The Ferris wheel failed to attract enough riders or cable car passengers, so after eight years on the North Side, it was shipped to St. Louis. The cars on the Ferris wheel are actually larger than the cable cars passing below. *Chicago Public Library, Northside Neighborhood History Collection.*

saw an opening. Behind the scenes, he bought a small portion of a subway line that would have been part of Morgan's proposed system, thereby blocking Morgan's entire proposal. Few people ever bested Morgan, who later described this as "the greatest rascality and conspiracy I ever heard of."

Yerkes proceeded with his plans, which were more colossal than anything he had yet undertaken. They included a powerhouse with eight 5,500-kilowatt turbine generators and four 275-foot chimneys to provide electricity to the existing subway and the three new lines.

The tough, determined Yerkes was partly driven by the realization that this work would make up much of his legacy because his health had begun to fail. He was suffering from nephritis, a kidney inflammation that, among other things, robbed him of his energy. By 1905, the disease had progressed to its final stages, sending Yerkes off into delusional fits. He did not live to see his London subways operating. He returned to New York and took up residence at the Waldorf-Astoria because his estranged wife would not allow him to return to his mansion.

Despised by his enemies but hailed by his allies, Charles Tyson Yerkes died on December 29, 1905. Near the end, his wife visited repeatedly, but so did the beautiful twenty-five-year-old Emilie Grigsby, whom Yerkes had taken under his wing toward the end of his life.

Yerkes's great wealth vanished with his passing because much of it was heavily leveraged or based on smoke and mirrors. Hard to understand during his life, Yerkes's finances were even harder to unravel after his death. Fights over his will dragged on for more than a decade.

Yerkes left his mansion and fabulous art collection, one of the finest private collections in the world, to New York. Alas, both had to be sold to pay off his debts, and the mansion was subsequently demolished. Yerkes's primary bequest was not to be a fabulous art collection or an elegant mansion to house it but rugged railway lines that continue to serve the transit needs of Chicagoans and Londoners to this day.

Theodore Dreiser immortalized Yerkes in his trilogy *The Financier*, *The Titan* and *The Stoic* loosely based on Yerkes's life.

Despite the cutting-edge transit facilities he bequeathed Chicago and London and the observatory he built for the University of Chicago, many critics were unforgiving of Yerkes, the "carpetbagging brigand." They picked his bones clean for moral and ethical lessons. One newspaper editorialist wrote that he had lived an "awful wreck of a life…The perversion of character, the complete absence of any guiding moral purpose and of a decent respect for the opinion of mankind leaves a heritage of shame to the nearest of kith and kin and a taint upon every item in the vast fortune. Out of the wreck we can make nothing but a warning."

Surprisingly, the *Chicago Tribune*, a paper that had vigorously criticized Yerkes throughout his Chicago tenure, was more appreciative of Yerkes's qualities and contributions: "Mr. Yerkes' notable career has come to an end and all animosities should be buried in his grave. While Chicagoans may regret that he was not more devoted to the public welfare than he was, they must admit his great ability and acknowledge that he contributed something to the progress of the city."

CHAPTER 8

CABLE CARS ON THE NORTH SIDE

Incorporated in 1859, the North Chicago City Railway built its first horsecar line that year by merely spiking rails to the city's plank road on Clark Street. The company grew slowly and became prosperous.

Throughout the 1860s, the North Side had fewer miles of horsecars in operation than the South or West Sides. Then the Great Chicago Fire of 1871 hit the North Chicago City Railway harder than other transit companies. Damage to CCR and the West Division Railway on the South and West Sides, respectively, was limited to their downtown trackage, but the fire destroyed most of North Chicago City Railway's trackage, cars and horses.

The company rebuilt after the fire, but its leaders were complacent, content with their steady stream of dividends. Low turnover in leadership and in the boardroom perpetuated the status quo. From 1859 until 1885, only two different men served as president and only seventeen men served on the company's board of directors. Even after CCR dramatically demonstrated in 1882 the advantages of cable car operations on heavily traveled lines in a flat city with cold winters, North Chicago City Railway showed no interest in going to the trouble or expense of investing in cable car technology. That would change once Charles Tyson Yerkes took over.

Soon after arriving in Chicago in 1881, Yerkes set his sights on transit. He identified street railways as a good way to make some serious money and a mark on history. His goal was to acquire all of Chicago's divergent street railways and unify them into a coherent, integrated network. Of course, he would benefit from the monopoly, but he also claimed his approach to transit would improve Chicago and set a standard for cities around the country.

His former partners—William Kemble, William Elkins and Peter Widener—were doing those things in Philadelphia. By 1881, they had gained control of much of that city's transit. Impressed with Chicago's South Side cable car installation, they began to convert to cable in 1883, making Philadelphia just the third U.S. city to have cable cars.

Yerkes wanted to buy one of Chicago's three major street railway companies and install cable cars, but none was for sale at that time. Nor did he have the funds. Yerkes had to bide his time.

In 1885, the first problem was solved when Voluntine Turner, North Chicago City Railway's president, decided to sell his 1,786 shares of the company, 36 percent of the total. The elderly widower needed money to build a mansion for his new fiancée. Yerkes tried unsuccessfully to raise money locally to buy out Turner, but Chicago's business leaders did not trust the newcomer, who had served time in prison.

A NCSR cable train on Lincoln Avenue nears the end of the line at Wrightwood Avenue. Professional photographers often photographed trainmen and later returned to sell them prints or postcards. The seats on this trailer did not reverse, so passengers sat face to face. *Chicago History Museum.*

Yerkes had little choice but to approach his well-heeled former partners in Philadelphia. Even though he had fallen out with them, Yerkes swallowed his pride and asked them to join him in a syndicate (a word that today may have criminal connotations but was used then for a legitimate business combination) to purchase North Chicago City Railway. Having made a fortune on transit in Philadelphia, the trio agreed, borrowed $1.5 million and made it available to Yerkes. By buying Turner's shares and 729 additional shares from another source, Yerkes acquired a bare majority of total shares—all that he needed to gain control of the company. The financier was on his way to becoming the Transit Titan, even though North Chicago City Railway was the runt of the litter of Chicago's three major transit companies.

A few days after the transactions were completed, the syndicate created a new company, North Chicago Street Railroad (NCSR), which leased North Chicago City Railway's property and named Yerkes president. The new company issued $1.5 million in bonds and used the money to pay back the loan. Thus, Yerkes and his partners gained control of the street railway without investing any of their own money. Over the years, Yerkes was to demonstrate that he had "an unlimited faith in his own power of achievement," as one writer put it in 1907. "Always alert and bold, he made his opportunity and executed his designs with an aggressive and unscrupulous hand."

Creating a new business entity erected an additional layer of corporate ownership and allowed Yerkes to obfuscate his financial manipulations and legal maneuverings. It also gave him more control and freedom to pursue his plans, which included first and foremost something that the staid previous owners of the North Side railway probably never would have undertaken: installing cable cars.

✂◯℞

Before building cable lines on the North Side, the transit company had to solve the bridge problem. In the 1880s, much of Chicago's commerce was waterborne, using docks along the Chicago River's main stem and branches. The few bridges that crossed the river were often crowded and created traffic bottlenecks on the streets. Rotated by steam power, the bridges were slow to open and close. During most of the year, they were open as much as one-quarter of the time to permit boats to pass.

Since cable cars could not feasibly cross a movable bridge, Yerkes proposed using a decrepit vehicular tunnel at LaSalle Street for the cable lines he intended to install. Built in 1871, the 30-foot-wide by 15-foot-9-inch-high public tunnel ran 1,890 feet from Michigan (now Hubbard) Street to Randolph Street. Heralded at its opening as "well lighted with gas, well ventilated and as neat, clean and free from dampness as could be desired," the tunnel had fallen into disrepair and was hardly ever used.

In June 1886, the City Council granted NCSR permission to use the old tunnel for $120,000. It also allowed the company to convert all of its horsecar lines to cable, provided that the street railway obtain consents from property owners along each route. Critics cried foul, accusing the aldermen of accepting bribes for their accord. The *Chicago Tribune* called the deal "a present of $600,000 worth of public property to Yerkes' car company in the shape of the LaSalle Street tunnel."

Mayor Harrison Sr. vetoed the "tunnel grab" ordinance, even though North Siders had been clamoring for cable service. In July 1886, he signed an alternative ordinance that allowed NCSR to convert all of its horsecar lines to cable and use the tunnel. In exchange, NCSR had to lower and rehabilitate the LaSalle Street tunnel, as well as relocate the Wells Street bridge to Dearborn Street and build new bridges at Wells and Clark Streets.

NCSR accepted the conditions and hired United States Construction, a company controlled by Yerkes, Widener and Elkins, to build its cable lines. Although it cost about $3 million to build NCSR's initial cable lines, the railway paid U.S. Construction $6 million in stocks, bonds and cash.

Yerkes and his lieutenants kept the wheels of government well greased and raised ever more capital by watering the stock of his new company. (This refers to issuing and selling more stock in a company than the company is worth.)

Conversion to cable began on Clark Street in September 1886. Myriad problems, including the weather, frontage consents, political challenges, legal injunctions and attempted shakedowns, delayed the work. Construction cost about $65,000 per mile of single track, not counting the expense of moving and/or enlarging underground electrical conduits and sewer, water and gas pipes.

One water main threatened to block all of Yerkes's plans. The main had to be relocated to make way for the cable car conduit, but doing so would require shutting down Chicago's water for one day, something that never would have been allowed. Instead, the indomitable Yerkes devised a solution, ordering a large number of specially curved metal bars that were used to divert the water. "I had to have those curves, and the expense was a consideration that did not enter into my mind," he said.

After lengthy delays, NCSR began operating cable cars on March 26, 1888, with a gala ceremony. The initial line ran on Clark Street from the so-called Limits car barn

Opposite: The North Side did not get cable cars until 1888, after Charles Tyson Yerkes took control of transit there and secured permission to use an abandoned but strategically located tunnel under the Chicago River. *Roy G. Benedict | Publishers' Services.*

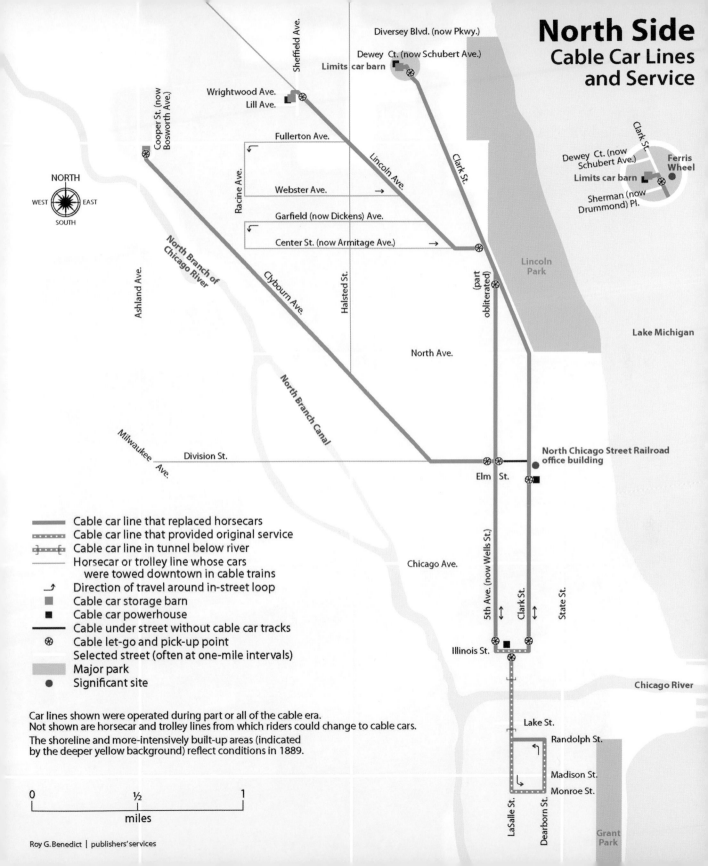

North Side
Cable Car Lines and Service

Diversey Blvd. (now Pkwy.)

Dewey Ct. (now Schubert Ave.)

Limits car barn

Sheffield Ave.

Wrightwood Ave.
Lill Ave.

Cooper St. (now Bosworth Ave.)

Clark St.

Dewey Ct. (now Schubert Ave.)

Limits car barn

Sherman (now Drummond) Pl.

Ferris Wheel

Fullerton Ave.

Racine Ave.

Webster Ave.

Lincoln Ave.

Garfield (now Dickens) Ave.

Center St. (now Armitage Ave.)

Lincoln Park

NORTH
WEST   EAST
SOUTH

North Branch of Chicago River

Clybourn Ave.

Halsted St.

(part obliterated)

Lake Michigan

Ashland Ave.

North Ave.

North Branch Canal

Milwaukee Ave.

Division St.

Elm   St.

North Chicago Street Railroad office building

Chicago Ave.

5th Ave. (now Wells St.)

Clark St.

State St.

Cable car line that replaced horsecars
Cable car line that provided original service
Cable car line in tunnel below river
Horsecar or trolley line whose cars
    were towed downtown in cable trains
↱ Direction of travel around in-street loop
▦ Cable car storage barn
■ Cable car powerhouse
    Cable under street without cable car tracks
⊗ Cable let-go and pick-up point
    Selected street (often at one-mile intervals)
    Major park
● Significant site

Illinois St.

Lake St.

Randolph St.

Madison St.
Monroe St.

LaSalle St.

Dearborn St.

Grant Park

Chicago River

Car lines shown were operated during part or all of the cable era.
Not shown are horsecar and trolley lines from which riders could change to cable cars.

The shoreline and more-intensively built-up areas (indicated
by the deeper yellow background) reflect conditions in 1889.

0   ½   1
miles

Roy G. Benedict | publishers' services

In September 1906, a southbound Wells Street cable train emerges from the LaSalle Street tunnel while a northbound Clark Street cable train enters. A sign saying "Electricity Is Life" portends the conversion to trolley service that was completed the following month. *Chicago Transit Authority.*

(near the city limits at that time) south of Diversey Avenue to Wisconsin Street. From there it split, continuing south on both Clark Street and 5th Avenue (now Wells Street). The lines rejoined at Illinois Street and continued south through the restored LaSalle Street tunnel and around a single-track downtown loop. The roundtrip took about fifty-six minutes.

Originally, the City Council allowed for a loop that included a section on Jackson Boulevard, but property owners on that street objected to cable cars, as they had previously to horsecars. Therefore, the single-track downtown loop ran from LaSalle and Randolph Streets, south to Monroe Street, east to Dearborn Street, north to Randolph Street and west back to its starting point. This limited the line's reach downtown.

NCSR kept building. In January 1889, it opened a cable branch on Lincoln Avenue. The ordinance that gave Yerkes the right to convert horsecar lines to cable lines included a clause that prohibited his railway from building a cable line on Clybourn Avenue because merchants on that street thought it would hurt their businesses. After they saw how cable increased business and property values on Clark Street, however, they asked Yerkes to proceed. The Clybourn Avenue line opened in 1891.

Inside the terminal at Clybourn Avenue and Cooper Street (now Bosworth Avenue), NCSR built a turntable rather than a loop or switchback for reversing cars. This was Chicago's only turntable used to reverse the direction of each cable car and train on a line. (Other car barns had smaller turntables for assembling cars into trains or moving them onto storage tracks.)

Cables on Clybourn Avenue and Clark and Wells Streets were driven from a powerhouse at Clark and Elm Streets that had previously housed a swimming pool and ice-skating rink. The cable for the Lincoln Avenue line was driven from a powerhouse at Lincoln and Wrightwood Avenues. And the cable that pulled trains through NCSR's troublesome downtown loop was driven from a powerhouse at LaSalle and Illinois Streets. (Although modified, this building is the most prominent remnant of Chicago's cable car system. It housed Michael Jordan's Restaurant and today is the home of LaSalle Power Co., a multilevel entertainment venue.)

Operation of the 9,670-foot downtown cable was a headache from day one. The cable's run included at least twelve right-angle turns. A malfunction of any of the cable's 320 underground curve pulleys brought the line to a halt. The LaSalle Street tunnel was the most problematic section of this run. The damp and dingy tunnel leaked. A steep grade (by Chicago standards) of 7 percent on each of the approaches was difficult to negotiate, needing extra power to ascend.

Exposed electrical wires ran the length of the tunnel above each track. Grip cars that traversed the tunnel were equipped with a curious three-foot trolley pole to draw that electricity—not to power the train but to light the interior of its cars.

Although modified, this former cable car powerhouse at LaSalle and Illinois Streets was designated a Chicago Landmark in 2001. It is the most prominent remnant of Chicago's cable car era and used to house Michael Jordan's Restaurant. *Photo by Jonathan Michael Johnson.*

Exceptionally heavy traffic levels taxed the entire system, especially the tunnel and loop. On the first day of operation, NCSR discovered to its horror that only about one of four cable trains could coast through the let-go turns at LaSalle and Illinois Streets on their own momentum. Therefore, it used teams of horses to pull each train through the turn to its pick-up point. This was expensive and caused tremendous delays. The company also discovered that the powerhouse at LaSalle and Illinois Streets did not have enough power to pull trains around the loop, so its power capacity had to be increased.

The first cables on this downtown loop lasted only one month due to the excessive wear and tear. As the cables stretched, they became thinner, so some grips were not tight enough to pull the train out of the tunnel. Soon, the company installed a new loop cable that was one and a half inches in diameter, the thickest cable ever used in Chicago. Life expectancy on this cable rose to seventy-four days, still only half that of cables on other lines.

Another problem at NCSR was the grip that the company selected. When installing cable lines in 1883 and again in 1885, the Philadelphia Traction Company used a top

A postcard of a northbound NCSR cable train on Dearborn Street crossing behind an eastbound WCSR cable train on Madison Street. Seniority gave superiority, so WCSR had to go to the expense and trouble of passing its cable under that of the previously installed cable of NCSR's line.

grip designed by Joel Low and Abraham Grim. This grip was hard on the cable and required new pads to be installed every three or four days. Worse, it required a long distance between cable let-go and pick-up points, which was especially challenging in flat cities such as Philadelphia and Chicago.

Rather than learning lessons from Philadelphia Traction's mistake with the aptly named Low and Grim grip, NCSR became the second—and only other—street railway to use this problematic grip. This shortsighted, money-saving venture resulted in some of the most difficult-to-operate cable lines in the country. The resulting poor service not only cost NCSR money but also created ill will with riders and soured the public on Yerkes. One typical complaint said, "The whole North Side is virtually up in arms against what is known as the 'Philadelphia Syndicate.'…it is a complete failure owing to the cheapness of the system put in. Delays are frequent and many are wishing for a return to horse power."

In addition to erring with its grip, NCSR made a curious decision when it introduced long, eight-wheel combination cars to Chicago. These new cars had seats for six or eight passengers on the open front platform and thirty more seats in the enclosed main section. They were superior in many respects, in particular because the control levers were located in the front of the car, thereby giving the gripman better forward visibility than the usual design that placed him in the middle of the grip car. Unfortunately, these thirty-foot cars were too long to negotiate the loop at the Limits car barn. Therefore, some of these cars were cut in two, resulting in a closed trailer and an open, twelve-foot-long grip car, the shortest grip cars ever operated in Chicago.

&⃝⃝&

At its peak of cable operations, NCSR had 8.5 miles of double track, 177 grip cars and an unknown number of trailers (probably 400 to 600). Its three powerhouses pulled nine separate cables. (For a few years, an additional engine in the Limits car barn probably powered one of these cables.) The company was managed from its headquarters at 444 N. Clark Street, later at 1165 N. Clark Street, a three-story office building fronting half of a block on Division Street.

NCSR was profitable during the cable car era. From 1893 to 1897, inclusive, it paid its stockholders an average dividend of 25 percent per year. In 1898, when its cars traveled more than ten million miles, the company earned $1.6 million on revenue of $30 million.

On the downside, the company was extremely overcapitalized. In 1897, NCSR's assets (including those of North Chicago City Railway, with which it was still financially

A southbound cable train on Clark Street passes an Oldsmobile on what is thought to be the last day of NCSR's cable car operation on Clark Street in 1906. *Chicago Public Library, Northside Neighborhood History Collection.*

intertwined) totaled $17.3 million, and its liabilities totaled $16.6 million. That left only $760,000 in net assets to represent $7.1 million in outstanding capital stock. Watering stocks in this fashion was yet another way Yerkes and his partners enriched themselves, in this case at the expense of their stockholders.

CHAPTER 9

CABLE CARS ON THE WEST SIDE

West Chicago Street Railroad (WCSR) did not begin operating cable cars until 1890, very late in the development of this initially promising mode of transit and well after some transit operators had already declared the electric trolley advantageous on virtually every front. The company's cable operations were burdened by a series of engineering, regulatory, operational and legal problems. The company cut corners in design and construction and operated two separate systems utilizing different, noncompatible grips. Aldermen tried to extort money, and merchants used cable car plans and routes to compete with one another.

Once launched, unusual route features created a drag on operations. These included two troublesome tunnels under the South Branch of the Chicago River, one of which had to be built from scratch; five of Chicago's six cable car crossings; and three loops, two of which had six right-angle turns through congested downtown areas.

Nevertheless, under Yerkes's direction, WCSR built cable lines with such gusto—some would say abandon—that it became the second-largest cable car company in the country, second only to the Chicago City Railway. It grew to include 15.2 miles of double track; six powerhouses (one of which was temporary); twelve cables; four routes; 230 grip cars and two to four times as many trailers; and Chicago's grandest cable car office building, a six-story structure with a clock tower at 12th Street and Blue Island Avenue. In 1893, its peak year for cable ridership, WCSR carried forty-six million cable car passengers.

ളൂര

The Chicago West Division Railway was incorporated on February 21, 1861, and began operating horsecars two years later when it purchased two routes from CCR. Over the next twenty-four years, the company built additional horsecar lines throughout the fan-shaped West Side. These lines reached as far as five miles west, and most of them converged downtown.

By the mid-1880s, the West Side had developed into the largest, most populous and fastest-growing section of Chicago. Still, it contained the poorest sections and endured the worst transportation services the city had to offer.

Soon after CCR introduced cable cars on the South Side in 1882, West Siders began clamoring for cable car service. At this time, most Chicago newspapers still reported favorably on cable cars, and West Siders wanted the newest thing in transit as much as anyone else did.

The stodgy Chicago West Division Railway directors turned a deaf ear to such pleas. The entrenched "aggregation of gray heads and feeble bodies," according to the *Chicago Times*, did not want to put their large profits at risk by changing the status quo. Added a financial observer at the time, "All they wanted was their

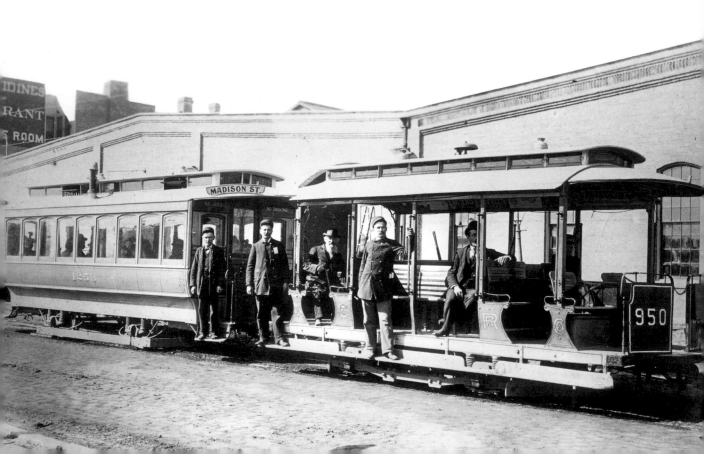

dividends, and they didn't want to do anything to improve their lines because it would cost money."

Given such attitudes, the Chicago West Division Railway was ripe for takeover. In control of transit on the North Side since 1895, Charles Tyson Yerkes had a master plan to gain control of all of Chicago's street railways, update the technology and combine them into one integrated system—pocketing a fortune along the way. Through creative financing, Yerkes and his Philadelphia partners had purchased the North Side transit system without investing a dime of their own money. They set out to use the same scheme on the West Side. The profits would be even bigger this time.

Yerkes's first overture to purchase a controlling interest in the Chicago West Division Railway in 1886 failed, but he succeeded one year later. His offer was just too tempting to turn down: $4 million, paid over two years, for a bare majority of the company's stock and a promise of 35 percent yearly dividends to the owners of the rest of the stock. After closing the deal, Yerkes created a new company, WCSR, and issued $4 million in bonds that covered the entire cost of the acquisition. Additional bonds were issued to cover the cost of constructing cable lines, and additional stock was sold for the personal benefit of Yerkes and his backers.

To counter the increasingly loud charge that he was an outsider, Yerkes was determined to include local investors in this transaction. He enticed four leading businessmen by giving them a free share of stock in the new company for every dollar's worth of bonds they purchased. Marshall Field, George Pullman, Levi Leiter and Nathaniel Fairbank each ponied up $400,000. The value of WCSR's stock rose, and two of them later sold their stock for $800,000 each—pure profit since they had acquired their shares for nothing.

At the same time, Yerkes purchased the Chicago Passenger Railway, a horsecar company that had been created in 1885 to compete with the Chicago West Division Railway. He combined Chicago Passenger Railway and WCSR and was now the master of transit on the West Side, as well as the North Side.

Throughout these financial machinations, the public din for cable on the West Side grew louder. Local politicians took notice. In June 1887, the City Council appointed a committee to consult with WCSR officials about converting horsecar lines to cable.

One of the hang-ups was access to the city center. As had been the case on the North Side, one or more tunnels would be needed to cross the river. Downtown bridges were

Opposite: A Madison Street cable train in front of the car barn at the end of the line near Springfield Avenue in the early 1890s. From left to right, the crewmen are the trailer conductor Swan Johnson, grip car conductor F.E. Daum and gripman Ed. Prowdy.

frequently open to allow river traffic to pass, and cables could not be strung over a movable bridge. A city-owned tunnel ran under the South Branch at Washington Street. Built in 1869 for vehicles and pedestrians, this tunnel had fallen into disrepair and was closed as unsafe. In 1884, a city engineer described it as "unsatisfactory," adding that "the leaking from the river continues, and it is not possible to stop it."

The City Council proposed that in exchange for permission to use the Washington Street tunnel and convert horsecar lines to cable, WCSR would have to pay for new bridges over the river, pave the full width of streets wherever cable was laid, reduce its fare and lower the tunnels to allow larger ships to pass overhead, as well as other conditions. Knowing the drill from having negotiated his way through a similar situation on the North Side, Yerkes refused to accept these conditions. Surmising that he had the upper hand, the Transit Titan waited out the situation.

The April 1888 elections demonstrated the shrewdness of this strategy. The public outcry for cable had grown louder, and West Side voters blamed not Yerkes but the incumbent aldermen for the fact that they were being deprived of cable car service. On election day, the voters swept out of office most of the aldermen who had opposed cable cars on the West Side or made excessive demands on WCSR.

Above: The western entrance to the Washington Street vehicular and pedestrian tunnel under the South Branch of the Chicago River shortly after it was built in 1869. Photo taken from near Clinton Street looking east. WCSR converted this tunnel to cable car operation. *Chicago History Museum*.

Opposite: The West Side was the last part of town to get cable cars, but WCSR made up for that with a vengeance. *Roy G. Benedict | Publishers' Services*.

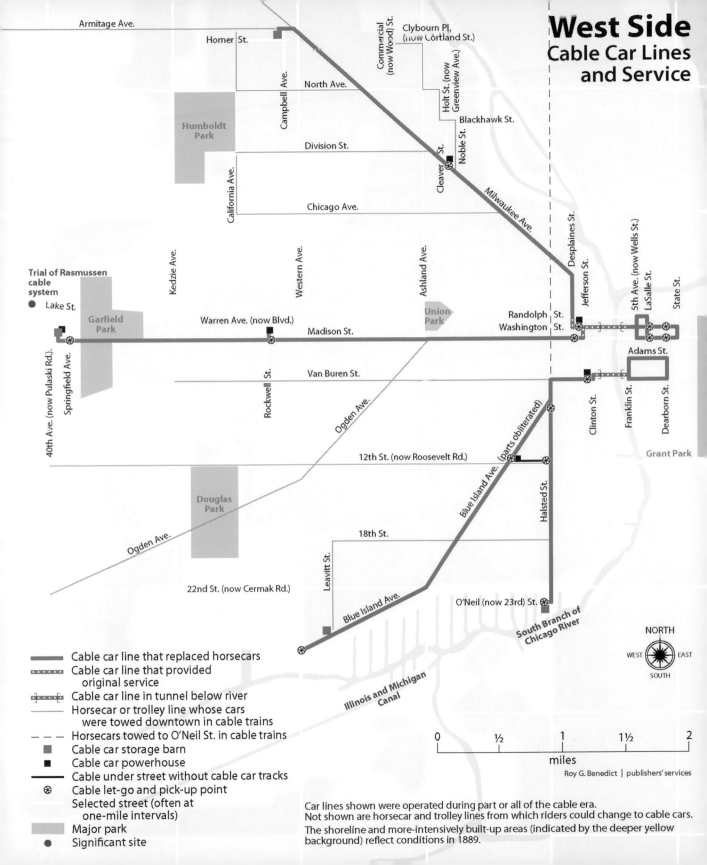

West Side
Cable Car Lines and Service

Armitage Ave.

Homer St.

Commercial (now Wood) St.

Clybourn Pl. (now Cortland St.)

Holt St. (now Greenview Ave.)

Blackhawk St.

North Ave.

Campbell Ave.

Humboldt Park

Division St.

California Ave.

Chicago Ave.

Cleaver St.

Noble St.

Milwaukee Ave.

Desplaines St.

Jefferson St.

5th Ave. (now Wells St.)

LaSalle St.

State St.

Kedzie Ave.

Western Ave.

Ashland Ave.

Union Park

Randolph St.

Washington St.

Trial of Rasmussen cable system

● Lake St.

Garfield Park

Warren Ave. (now Blvd.)

Madison St.

Springfield Ave.

40th Ave. (now Pulaski Rd.)

Adams St.

Rockwell St.

Van Buren St.

Ogden Ave.

12th St. (now Roosevelt Rd.)

Blue Island Ave. (parts obliterated)

Clinton St.

Franklin St.

Dearborn St.

Grant Park

Halsted St.

Douglas Park

18th St.

Leavitt St.

Ogden Ave.

22nd St. (now Cermak Rd.)

Blue Island Ave.

O'Neil (now 23rd) St.

South Branch of Chicago River

Illinois and Michigan Canal

NORTH
WEST EAST
SOUTH

Legend

— Cable car line that replaced horsecars

··· Cable car line that provided original service

▥ Cable car line in tunnel below river

— Horsecar or trolley line whose cars were towed downtown in cable trains

-- Horsecars towed to O'Neil St. in cable trains

▪ Cable car storage barn

■ Cable car powerhouse

— Cable under street without cable car tracks

⊗ Cable let-go and pick-up point

Selected street (often at one-mile intervals)

Major park

● Significant site

0   ½   1   1½   2
miles

Roy G. Benedict | publishers' services

Car lines shown were operated during part or all of the cable era.
Not shown are horsecar and trolley lines from which riders could change to cable cars.
The shoreline and more-intensively built-up areas (indicated by the deeper yellow background) reflect conditions in 1889.

The City Council quickly passed a cable car ordinance with more favorable conditions, and Yerkes accepted the bill's less arduous requirements that he rebuild the tunnel and pay most of the cost for building a new bridge at Washington Street. With considerable foresight, the ordinance allowed WCSR to convert any of its existing lines from horse to cable *or* electric power. The handwriting was on the wall.

As North Chicago Street Railroad had done, WCSR contracted with United States Construction, which was controlled by Yerkes's syndicate, to build its first cable line— and paid the company twice the value of the work. Construction began in the summer of 1888 but proceeded slowly.

The Washington Street tunnel, which had to be lowered to allow ever-larger ships on the Chicago River to pass, cost $200,000 to refurbish and convert to cable. Grain merchants and the Board of Trade, both of which stood to gain from a deeper shipping channel, might have contributed to the expense or cooperated with the work. Instead, they fought the changes in state and federal courts. They objected to the fact that only

The signal tower in front of the powerhouse at Washington and Jefferson Streets controlled the switch where the Milwaukee Avenue and Madison Street cable lines intersected. A wreck wagon on the right stands ready to rush to the scene of a crash. This building is now the headquarters of the International Brotherhood of Electrical Workers, Local 134. *Courtesy of the International Brotherhood of Electrical Workers.*

half the width of the river would be available for shipping during construction. WCSR prevailed in court, but this dispute delayed commencement of cable car service.

One thing WCSR did right was to heed lessons learned from the troubled, cost-cutting design and construction of NCSR's cable lines. For example, rather than using the obdurate Low and Grim top grip, WCSR used a side grip.

Service was finally inaugurated on Milwaukee Avenue on June 18, 1890, between the terminus at Armitage Avenue and the powerhouse at Cleaver Street, where two one-hundred-horsepower engines issued the two cables that pulled these trains. Soon the line was extended southeast to Washington and Jefferson Streets.

Shortly thereafter, service commenced on the Madison Street line. A powerhouse at Rockwell Street equipped with two one-thousand-horsepower engines issued the two cables that pulled these trains.

On Milwaukee Avenue, WCSR used primarily large, double-truck, eight-wheel combination cars. These single-ended cars had to be turned at the end of the line, which was accomplished with a turnaround loop in the Armitage Avenue car barn at the end of the line. (Most North and West Side terminal car barns had such turning loops.) On Madison Street, WCSR used small, open, four-wheel grip cars pulling one or more trailers. These cars were reversed for their return trip via a turnaround loop at the terminal car barn near Springfield Avenue.

෯෨

WCSR's initial two lines were operationally challenged. Trains on the 4.5-mile Milwaukee Avenue route depended on four different cables, while trains on the 5.2-mile Madison Street route depended on five different cables. Problems on any one cable shut down that entire line.

The busy intersection of the Milwaukee Avenue and Madison Street lines at Washington and Jefferson Streets required a flagman to operate the switch located there. In 1891, WCSR installed a Chicago rarity at this corner: a fifteen-foot tower from which an employee operated the switch for the two cable lines using the force of compressed air. The tower also provided a signal with colored signs during the day and colored lanterns at night to indicate which train had clearance. Such towers allowed faster switching and kept the switchmen out of the often-busy street traffic.

In August 1890, a clean, refurbished and brightly lit Washington Street tunnel opened, thereby allowing WCSR's cable trains access to downtown. WCSR's first downtown loop ran from Washington Street and Fifth Avenue (now Wells Street) south to Madison Street, east to LaSalle Street, north to Randolph Street, west to Fifth Avenue and south back to its starting point. Both the Milwaukee Avenue and

Madison Street cable lines shared the tunnel and loop. A powerhouse at Washington and Jefferson Streets drove both loop cables.

The loop's six right-angle corners slowed trains, created traffic bottlenecks and prematurely wore out the cable. In addition, the loop operated on the left hand side of LaSalle Street—contrary to the flow of traffic.

Another problem was that the loop stopped three blocks short of State Street, then a shopping mecca and the center of Chicago's business district. This was not by design. WCSR had planned to locate the eastern side of this loop on State Street, where WCSR already ran horsecars, but two factors forced it to use LaSalle Street instead: the City Council's refusal to grant WCSR permission to operate cable cars on State Street and a disagreement with CCR's President Holmes over cable routes.

Massive cable infrastructure was so expensive that companies rarely went to the trouble of rerouting a line. Both WCSR and CCR, however, decided that rerouting their downtown loops would be worth the expense. While WCSR sought cable car access to State Street, CCR sought better operating efficiency downtown for its two cable lines. Realizing that it was a mistake to operate both its lines on one crowded loop, CCR wanted to reroute its Cottage Grove Avenue cable line along a new second loop that would include Michigan Avenue. To do this, it needed permission from WCSR, which held a franchise on that street.

Yerkes offered CCR rights to Michigan Avenue in exchange for rights to State Street, but Holmes demanded money in addition, reportedly as much as $800,000. The two men continued to negotiate. Ironically, Yerkes had allies on this issue at CCR. State Street merchants on CCR's board wanted West Side residents to have easy access to their stores. The most prominent was Leiter, who led Holmes's ouster from CCR in January 1891. That cleared the path, once again, for Yerkes to get his way and extend his downtown loop eastward.

The City Council approved WCSR's desired route for its new loop in March 1892, and construction began soon thereafter. Nevertheless, the newly configured loop did not open until November 1893 due to construction delays. It ran from Washington Street and Fifth Avenue (now Wells Street) south to Madison Street, east to State Street, north to Washington Street and west back to its starting point. Both the Milwaukee Avenue and Madison Street cable lines used the new loop. The powerhouse at Washington and Jefferson Streets drove both loop cables. The ten-mile roundtrip on the Milwaukee Avenue line took ninety-five minutes and operated at fourteen miles per hour. The nine-mile roundtrip on the Madison Street line took seventy-four minutes and operated at twelve miles per hour.

While WCSR's new loop provided several advantages—not least the fact that it had only four rather than six right-angle turns—it also had disadvantages. It had to

Looking east on Madison Street at 5th Avenue (now Wells Street) as a cable train takes a turn on one of WCSR's three downtown cable car loops. This combination grip car is pulling a North Avenue horsecar. The sentry box on the right topped off with a light is a police box that was used to communicate with the police station. *Chicago History Museum.*

cross NCSR cable car tracks four times and its own tracks once. As the newcomer, or "junior" line, WCSR had to bear the costs of engineering and constructing the complicated intersections with NCSR. Also, it had to ensure that its grips would not slice the "senior" line's cable or otherwise damage NCSR equipment.

NCSR wrestled over crossings with intercity railroads as well. In the 1890s, the city pressured steam railroads to elevate their lines to avoid the danger of operating at street level. The railroads did not always comply with these orders; sometimes they did so begrudgingly. In 1897, more than one railroad had tracks running through the intersection of Rockwell and Madison Streets. They raised their tracks but only nine feet above street level, which blocked the cable cars on Madison Street. WCSR had to pay to lower Madison Street so that its cable cars could pass below the new railroad overpass. To do this, it had to remove the foundations, conduits and vaults that had

A Blue Island Avenue cable train approaches Ashland Avenue and 22nd Street in 1905. The grip carries ads for *The Geezer of Geck* at the Garrick Theater and fireworks at Paul Boyton's Water Chute, America's first modern amusement park. Overhead wires and utility poles were unsightly, even prior to the construction of trolley lines. *Chicago History Museum.*

been installed only a few years earlier under and around its powerhouse at Rockwell and Madison Streets.

These crossings also created operational challenges for NCSR. Gripmen had to drop the cable at precisely the correct moment to be able to coast through these intersections and then pick up the cable, which often proved troublesome. When a car did not coast all the way through the intersection, the conductor had to push it the rest of the way, typically with the help of male passengers.

ഒരു

Even though time was running out on cable cars by the early 1890s, WCSR continued its aggressive stance regarding this technology. After the fact, it is easy to say that WCSR should have known better. Nevertheless, it proceeded headstrong, planning and constructing two new lines, one on Blue Island Avenue and another on Halsted Street.

Construction began in July 1891, but the slow delivery of cable equipment and machinery delayed the work. When WCSR discovered that the powerhouse at Blue Island Avenue and 12th Street (now Roosevelt Road) was being constructed on quicksand, the foundation had to be extended forty feet underground, which reportedly required a million bricks.

Service on the Blue Island Avenue line finally began on July 27, 1893. Initially, the line ran from Western Avenue and Blue Island Avenue to Jefferson and Van Buren Streets. The Halsted Street line began service on August 24, 1893, running from Halsted and O'Neil Streets to Jefferson and Van Buren Streets. Downtown access would have to wait for the completion of WCSR's second tunnel.

•••

As with WCSR's first two cable lines, crossing the river to get downtown was vital but problematic for its second two lines. For the two new lines, WCSR had to build a tunnel, which turned out to be Chicago's only privately owned cable car tunnel. After land was purchased and injunctions meant to stop the tunnel or bilk the company were overcome, work began in February 1890. Amazingly, it took four years and $1.5 million to complete the tunnel.

In a unique arrangement for Chicago, the tunnel ran on and under private property 150 feet north of Van Buren Street between Clinton and Franklin Streets. Several buildings had to be demolished; others were rebuilt after the track work and approaches were completed.

Because the tunnel was only 1,500 feet long, steep grades of 10 to 12 percent were required to pass below the river. The sharp decline and incline, which required a special emergency braking system to be installed in the tracks, would plague this tunnel during its short life.

The emergency brakes came in handy on December 14, 1894, when a heavily loaded three-car train slid back into the tunnel after its grip broke. The passengers panicked and began jumping off the train. The conductor applied the emergency brake, but the sudden jolt knocked passengers to the floor, injuring several of them. After the following cable train failed to push the incapacitated train out of the tunnel, a wreck-wagon crew cleaned up the mess. Service was restored in less than one hour, the *Chicago Tribune* reported. "Had it not been for the emergency brake, which works on a cog in the center of the track, the trainmen say a disaster…might have ensued."

•••

Crossing the river was one thing; looping through downtown was another. The loop for the Blue Island Avenue and Halsted Street cable lines was the sixth and final one built downtown. Since the tunnel did not align with a street, six right-angle corners were unavoidable. Opening on April 21, 1894, the new loop ran from the eastern end of the tunnel at Franklin Street, south to Van Buren Street, east to Dearborn Street, north to Adams Street, west to Franklin Street and south back to the tunnel.

At a maximum speed of twelve miles per hour, the eight-mile roundtrip on the Blue Island Avenue cable line took about sixty-eight minutes. At a maximum speed of ten miles per hour, the six-mile roundtrip on the Halsted Street cable line took about fifty-eight minutes.

The following year, WCSR began to electrify its horsecar lines, starting with 18th Street. As they had done with horsecars, WCSR cable trains towed trolley cars from connecting lines through downtown until overhead wires were permitted in the city center. What an odd sight that must have been—an old, rickety, single-truck grip car pulling a new, larger, double-truck electric car with its temporarily useless trolley pole tied down on its roof.

Grip cars had great difficulty pulling loads of cable trailers up the steep incline of WCSR's Van Buren Street tunnel, and this problem was exacerbated when a heavy trolley car was attached to a cable train. WCSR tried to address this problem by replacing the soft metal grip pads with hard steel ones. Alas, the harder metal and the extra weight of the trolley car damaged the cable and caused more frequent breaks. As a result, the cable had to be replaced every seven days rather than every forty days.

A better solution was to use electricity to help push a cable train through the tunnel. To accomplish this unusual maneuver, the conductor attached the electric car's trolley pole to the overhead wire that was normally used to light cable car interiors. In this case, however, the electric power was used to boost the train forward. "The novel sight is often seen of a motor car at the rear end of a [cable] train pushing while the grip car in front pulls ahead as usual," said the *Chicago Tribune* in November 1895.

A still better solution for powering trains through the tunnel was to electrify Chicago's street railway lines. WCSR wanted to do so but refused many of the conditions that the city insisted on. Yerkes could afford to wait for the city to change its tune. By this time, he controlled transit on both the North and West Sides, which gave him tremendous negotiating power.

In the end, WCSR was not able to convert its cable lines. That would happen years later under Chicago Union Traction, which Yerkes formed just before moving to New York in 1899 to merge WCSR and NCSR. Soon it became clear that Union Traction was a combination of underperforming firms burdened with crushing debt. In fact, Union Traction was practically insolvent from the day it was formed.

The massive cable car powerhouse at Van Buren and Jefferson Streets, seen here in 1962 when it was a Commonwealth Edison substation, drove the 9,800-foot cable for WCSR's southern downtown cable car loop. *Chicago History Museum.*

In 1903, the inevitable occurred: Union Traction fell into receivership after failing to meet its heavy liabilities.

This was the same year that most of Chicago's street railway franchises expired—at least according to some experts. The controversial topic was frequently debated in local newspapers and argued in court. No matter who was correct, the uncertainty made it nearly impossible to raise capital to improve cable car infrastructure or purchase sorely needed trolley cars. Having run for fifteen years, the "traction war" was not over yet. Transit companies insisted on converting their cable lines to trolley lines, experts

A WCSR cable train waiting to depart from the car barn on Blue Island Avenue at Leavitt Street in 1895. The building on the left in the background is now a factory, although it has been reduced to one story or its façade shortened. On the left is conductor Henry Kolley, and next to him is gripman L.L. Francoeur.

conducted studies, legislators introduced proposals, reformers held their ground and businessmen butted heads over the long-outstanding issues related to conversion, franchise duration, fees and public ownership of transit, which will be covered in the chapter on the demise of Chicago's cable cars.

In the meantime, suffice it to say that transit service deteriorated citywide during this protracted debate. The once popular cable car became a laughingstock, political football, media whipping boy and financial liability. Its demise was imminent.

CHAPTER 10

CHICAGO'S CABLE CAR MAIL SERVICE

In the 1890s and early 1900s, some mailboxes in Chicago weighed more than eight tons. These behemoths were, in fact, cable cars fitted with drop slots for mailing letters. They rolled all over town as part of the streetcar Railway Post Office (RPO) service.

On May 25, 1895, the West Chicago Street Railroad officially inaugurated Chicago's RPO service on Madison Street. Before the inaugural run, local politicians and post office dignitaries made speeches about how the mail would be carried across town better by cable cars than by the plodding horse-drawn wagons in service up until then. "The poor man will be able to have his letter…delivered as quickly as by special messenger!" declared Chicago Postmaster Washington Hesing.

WCSR's inaugural RPO service utilized a cable car specially built by the Pullman Palace Car Company. Trailer No. 1 was one of the most unusual RPO cable cars ever operated. One-third of the thirty-foot-long combination car was devoted to mail handling, including a worktable and 176 slots for sorting letters. The rest of the car was devoted to passenger seating.

The first route worked so well that a second cable car was added and the service extended. Soon, the route spanned five miles and employed five clerks. Before long, Chicago's three major transit companies were operating RPO routes using cable cars.

෩෧

The roots of streetcar RPOs go back to the 1830s, when intercity trains began carrying bags of mail. The practice became so common that in 1838 the U.S. Congress designated all railroad lines as postal routes. By the late 1850s, the volume of mail that mainline railroads carried had grown tremendously. George Armstrong, manager of the Chicago Post Office in the 1860s, suggested the idea of saving time by sorting mail onboard intercity trains as they traveled across the country. As a result, in 1864, the Chicago & North Western Railway began operating an RPO that sorted mail en route between Chicago and Clinton, Iowa. By 1890, 5,800 postal clerks were sorting mail over 154,800 miles of mainline railroads.

The following year, the concept of sorting mail en route was extended to street railways and tested in St. Louis. The novelty of the idea attracted media attention. "The windows of the postal compartment are protected by a wire netting, so that while the windows may be opened in warm weather there is no possibility of any of the mail being blown out of the windows," reported one newspaper.

Congress made the streetcar mail service official in 1894 by passing a bill that designated street railways as postal routes. The following year, it appropriated funds to operate streetcar RPOs in a number of cities, including Chicago. After WCSR

A CCR cable car converted for Railway Post Office service. Grip cars towed this trailer and others like it in Chicago from 1895 to 1901; then trolleys took over until 1915. The "blind" access-free end of this car was for security. Note the mail slot between the door and the eagle. *Chicago Public Library, Special Collections and Preservation Division.*

demonstrated the feasibility of streetcar mail service in Chicago, the Post Office Department contracted with the city's transit companies to operate RPO routes. The cars carried mail between post office stations and mail pouch pick-up locations. By the end of the following year, four cable car RPO routes, each with two cars, served ten Chicago stations, "advancing mail delivery by one to five hours," according to the *Chicago Tribune*. Soon thereafter, a fifth route was added, bringing the total mileage of Chicago's cable car RPOs to approximately forty-four miles (roundtrip). The dates below indicate estimated periods for cable car RPO operation; the mileage figures indicate round-trip route miles, most or all of which was by cable.

- Madison Street (1895–1901, 10.6 miles);
- Milwaukee Avenue (1895–1901, 8.4 miles);
- Clark Street and Lincoln Avenue (1895–96, 8.6 miles);
- Clark and Wells Streets (1896–1901, 7.6 miles, replacing the Clark Street and Lincoln Avenue route); and
- Wabash Avenue, 22nd Street and Cottage Grove Avenue (1896–1906, 16.6 miles).

By 1895, Chicago's mail delivery district covered 125 square miles and handled about two million pieces of mail daily. This gigantic task was difficult, especially given traffic congestion and the primitive state of Chicago's streets. Cable cars made the job speedier and more efficient. That year, the second assistant U.S. postmaster general reported, "The [cable car RPO] service has proved so satisfactory the short time it has been in force that it is recognized as a necessity." Transit companies in other cities, including San Francisco, Cincinnati and New York, also began operating cable car RPOs, the latter with ten dedicated cars.

Most of Chicago's RPO cable cars were converted horsecars, modified for mail service and fitted with mail drop slots. They were painted white, trimmed in red and blue and decorated with the U.S. Post Office Department eagle. Sometimes one of these mail trailers would be the only trailer pulled by a grip car; other times, one would be added to a passenger train in revenue service.

Typically, the cable car RPOs were staffed by one or two postal clerks who would exchange pouches with connecting RPO cable lines or at mail transfer points alongside the tracks. Mail had to be carted by horse between these transfer points and the local post office station.

As clerks sorted the mail on cable cars, they would often cancel it, time permitting. Today, streetcar RPO cancellations are prized collectors' items. Clear cancellations are especially rare, given the bumpy, rocky ride that streetcars typically delivered.

Chicago's cable car RPOs operated continuously from as early as 5:30 a.m. to after midnight, making as many as sixteen daily roundtrips, each one through a downtown cable car loop. The volume of mail grew rapidly, reaching enormous levels. Special

Cable car mail service covered forty-five route miles (roundtrip), including this section of Milwaukee Avenue looking northwest at Ashland Avenue in 1906. *Chicago Transit Authority.*

service was given to firms with high volumes of mail. The American School of Correspondence, a pioneer in the field of home study located in Hyde Park, could dump as many as seventy-five pouches of letters on a luckless crew at one time.

"The street car service has been an immense improvement undoubtedly on all preceding services," noted *A Review of the Postal Service in Chicago* by the Chicago postmaster, published in 1901. "It provides an hourly dispatch of mail to all stations on the lines and, in conjunction with the steam railroads, permits a complete and frequent interchange of mails during the day between all stations and [Chicago's] General Post Office."

This unbridled enthusiasm led post office personnel to speculate that the service would expand further. One predicted that the cable car service would replace all horse-drawn mail wagons. Another suggested that letter carriers would pick up their mail to be delivered directly from cable car RPOs and that locked mail pouches could be carried on any cable passenger train in revenue service.

All of this was not to be. Starting in 1901, trolley cars took over one cable car RPO route after another. In their turn, Chicago's trolley-based RPO routes developed into an extensive network of six routes serving more than forty post office stations spread over more than sixty route miles with an estimated twenty dedicated mail cars. Mail volume became extremely large. In 1909, just one Chicago trolley line carried 3,260 pouches of mail in a single day.

Next, the introduction of pneumatic *tubes* to move mail downtown in the late 1890s followed by the introduction of vehicles riding on pneumatic *tires* in the early 1900s supplanted trolley-based RPOs.

Chicago's streetcar mail service was discontinued on November 21, 1915, terminating a widely successful run of more than twenty years spanning both cable cars and trolleys. All told, fourteen U.S. cities provided streetcar mail service. Baltimore was the last city to give it up in 1929. Mainline intercity railroad RPOs, however, continued to operate until 1977.

CHAPTER 11

DEMISE OF CHICAGO'S CABLE CARS

For a technology that was obsolete shortly after being introduced, cable cars hung on for a surprising number of years in cities and towns around the country. By the late 1890s, the shortcomings of cable cars had become pronounced and undeniable. Trolleys had eclipsed them. Still, cable cars refused to disappear in Chicago until 1906, by which time their technology was outdated and their service derided.

Many factors contributed to this longevity. Investors who had poured some $25 million into the lines, cars and powerhouses were reluctant to give up on their investments. And once a system was built, operating it was relatively inexpensive, creating a disincentive to abandon heavily traveled cable lines. More important, converting horsecar lines to trolley lines offered bigger savings and was therefore more urgent than converting cable lines to trolley lines.

Politics and personality played roles, too. Waging a protracted traction war, politicians used their power over street railways and corporations to enrich themselves and garner votes. Chicago's leading businessmen locked horns over transit issues, and reformers blocked many changes on the assumption that transit companies were corrupt and not to be trusted.

From the horsecar days on, city and state politicians asserted control over what street railways could do. Their biggest control lever was their power to grant or deny franchises. For horsecar lines, franchises tended to be short, covering only twenty-five years. Even so, the city did not grant them lightly. "Whilst advantages may accrue to the city from the building and operating of horse railways, at the same time it will, I think, be conceded that the franchises are valuable. In handing them over to individuals, the public and private interests that are affected by this transfer should be most fully guarded and protected," said Mayor John Haines in 1858.

By 1883, a large number of the early twenty-five-year horsecar franchises were set to expire. With cable cars arriving on the scene, transit companies sought franchise extensions and longer franchises going forward. They argued that twenty-five years did not give them enough time to recoup the considerable investment that cable car technology required. Longer franchises proved elusive, however, as politicians and the public had grown increasingly distrustful of transit barons and their stockholders. In addition, there was uncertainty about the validity and duration of existing franchises; the vulnerability of street railways to fees and taxes; and even who had ultimate authority over street railways—the city or the state.

Aldermen took sides and demonstrated great skill in manipulating the issues to their own advantage. "Many deserving aldermen will be enabled to provide themselves against want next winter," the *Chicago Tribune* opined in 1883. Other newspapers described the City Council as "a thoroughly rotten and dishonest body, always for sale to the highest bidder," and as "a fetid, steaming, rotting morass."

Rather than resolving the streetcar franchise issue, the City Council in 1883 passed compromise legislation that extended existing franchises twenty years in exchange for transit companies paying the city fifty dollars per year per car. Mayor Harrison Sr., who brokered this deal, conceded that street railways "do not wish to be at the mercy of every new council to come in." This set the stage for a heated battle as 1903 approached.

By 1886, Yerkes had become the dominant force in Chicago transit and fought for longer franchises. As he assumed that mantle, he came to personify the Gilded Age transit baron whom the public had come to distrust and even revile. Social reformers fueled this ire, aiming much of their vitriol at transit companies, which they portrayed as "soulless monopolies." Reformers called for competition between street railways, but this was impractical, given how counterproductive it would have been to build competing cable lines along adjacent routes, argues Robert Weber in *Rationalizers and Reformers.* Reformers fought transit companies at every turn, even though the public would have been better served by stronger, more viable companies with longer franchises, more lines and through routes. This approach played a major role in saddling Chicago with disjointed, dysfunctional transit.

In fact, the reformers served the interest of private property owners and businessmen, many of whom were wealthy, at the expense of street railways that served a broad cross section of society, as Weber demonstrates in his excellent analysis. With a lack of rational thought and central planning, Chicago's transit developed willy-nilly, and cable car service remained fragmented and uncoordinated.

One of the most prominent reformers was William Stead, an English journalist who arrived in Chicago in 1893 and unleashed a popular campaign against corrupt

Experimentation with alternatives to cable traction continued throughout the 1890s. Compressed air cars were tried on Lake and Halsted Streets on the West Side circa 1890 and on the North Side from 1899 to 1906, primarily in night service when the cable was shut down. This compressed air train is at the Limits car barn on Clark Street.

politicians, bar and brothel owners—and transit companies. The cover of his 1894 book, *If Christ Came to Chicago*, depicts Yerkes scooping up money and clutching a cable car at the feet of Jesus, who is driving him and other tycoons away.

Rumblings about municipal ownership of transit added to the uncertainty created by short and expiring franchises. Car orders declined, maintenance was deferred and transit deteriorated further.

৯৫৫৫

In 1897, the Humphrey Bill was introduced in the state legislature. In exchange for fifty-year franchises, transit companies were to be taxed 1 to 7 percent of their gross receipts. This bill was defeated due to strong opposition from reformers, labor groups, newspapers and the public.

In its place, the legislature passed the Allen Bill, which ironically was more generous to street railways. It allowed for fifty-year franchises, permitted noncompeting transit companies to consolidate and included measures that would have made competition less likely. Furthermore, it did not tax street railways. Such generosity was probably bought; it was reported that the passage of the bill cost transit companies $500,000 in payoffs. Opposition in Chicago to the Allen Bill was widespread and well organized. The anti-Yerkes press stirred the pot, and aldermen supporting the measure were threatened with violence.

In January 1899, the City Council considered the legislature's Allen Bill. After opponents showed up in the gallery swinging nooses, the aldermen declared that the bill should be repealed. Ironically, public sentiments were so strong against the Allen Bill that Yerkes was forced to use his influence in Springfield to repeal it. It reportedly cost him as much in boodle to repeal the bill as it had cost him to pass it in the first place! It was repealed in March 1899, returning the situation to the status quo: twenty-five-year street railway franchises, many of which were set to expire in 1903.

Yerkes could see that reformers had gained the upper hand. Although he had made major progress toward achieving his goal of unifying Chicago transit, he sold off his holdings and moved to New York, as previously described.

Still, the traction war was not over. The federal government got involved in 1904 by declaring the cable car tunnels an obstruction to navigation. Chicago Union Traction offered to pay for lowering the tunnels in exchange for the right to install trolley wires downtown, and the City Council finally relented. In 1905–07, it passed a series of "Settlement Ordinances," which voters later approved. The settlement extended franchises, imposed various operating requirements on street railways and established a transit oversight body. It allowed for more consolidation and a more unified transit system. And it brought Chicago's cable car era to a close by requiring street railways to convert their cable car and horsecar lines to electricity. The traction war was finally over.

SEARCHING FOR AN ALTERNATIVE TO CABLE

So much for the role of politics and legislation in the prolonged life and ultimate demise of the cable car in Chicago. Now let's step back to the 1880s and follow the demise of the cable car in terms of technology. How and why did it fall from its pedestal? The experimentation with various forms of motive power for transit that preceded the introduction of cable cars intensified during the cable car era. Steam, gas, electricity and other forms of power were tested. Inventors developed battery-powered motors that propelled railcars over short distances, but the crude batteries available were unreliable and costly.

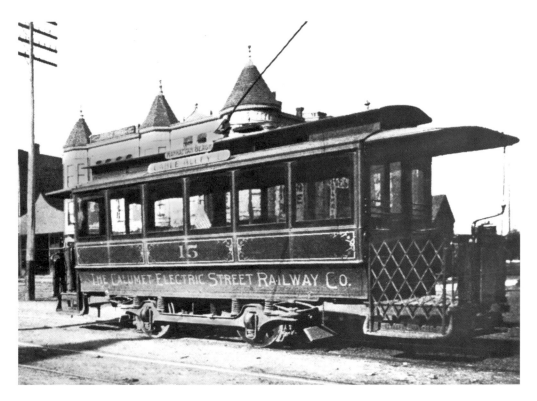

On October 2, 1890, the Calumet Electric Street Railway installed the first overhead trolley wires in Chicago. This successful company merged with the South Chicago City Railway in 1908.

Electrically powered streetcars became feasible only after 1870 with the development of a reliable dynamo, a machine that generates electricity. In 1881, Werner von Siemens devised a somewhat successful electric streetcar system near Berlin that relied on electric power transmitted through a rail to a motor underneath the car, but the exposed current was dangerous to pedestrians. In the early 1880s, Charles VanDepoele and Leo Daft addressed this safety concern by providing electric power from an overhead wire via a grooved wheel called a "troller" attached to a pole on top of the car. They were on to something, but their early trolleys were not dependable.

Trying to stave off the cable car's demise, many inventors attempted to improve its reliability and lower the prohibitive cost of constructing cable lines. They were not successful. For example, in 1887, Henry Casebolt built an experimental line in Oakland with an overhead cable moving on pulleys attached to poles alongside the track. Not having to build a conduit reduced costs, but the system did not operate well.

Chicago's Charles Rasmussen and others developed a system that used a shallow conduit and did away with the grip. It used sprocketed wheels about three feet in diameter on each car. The wheels reached through a slot in the track into the conduit where the sprockets would engage small buttons or collars attached to the cable every eight inches. Small sets of wheels that rode six feet apart on rails inside the conduit were attached to and carried the cable along. The sprocketed wheel in the car was free to spin. If the operator applied a handbrake to the wheel, however, the wheel stopped spinning, got caught on the buttons and propelled the car forward. The wheel could be added to any horsecar, and the simple conduit was relatively inexpensive to build, about $23,500 per double-track mile.

In 1886, the Rasmussen system was tested on Chicago West Division Railway (a predecessor of WCSR) on a stretch of Lake Street between 40th (now Pulaski Road) and 42nd (now Keeler) Avenues. The system did not function well because it concentrated great forces on the small area where each button was attached to the cable. Cable stretching and the slippage of buttons along the cable caused a misalignment between the sprockets and buttons.

As electricity emerged as the frontrunner in the race to replace cable cars, the continuing opposition to overhead wires downtown became a big hurdle. Overhead wires were considered dangerous, carrying, as they typically did, six hundred volts of direct current. If a live wire broke, it could electrocute pedestrians and horses or start a fire. Also, overhead wires could hinder firemen fighting a blaze.

In addition, overhead wires were considered unsightly. Yerkes himself had aesthetic reservations about overhead wires. "I saw the telephone and telegraph wires come down with pride," he said in 1899, "and was anxious when it appeared that electricity was the coming motive power that something else than the over-head trolley should be used in the business district."

To avoid overhead wires, the City Council asked Chicago's transit companies to operate trolleys using electrical wires buried underground, as in New York and Washington, D.C. Having struggled for years to build and maintain underground conduits for cable cars, the transit companies were not keen on this idea. Nevertheless, Yerkes and others gave it a try. For this, Yerkes turned, once again, to Philadelphia, where John Love had developed a system that functioned with a slot in the track through which a lever on the car was used to make contact with the underground electrical wires. In April 1892, Yerkes's North Chicago Street Railroad began operating two such cars on a 1½-mile single-track loop on Halsted Street and Fullerton, Racine and Webster Avenues.

The scheme failed miserably. In hot weather, the wires expanded and short-circuited; in cold weather, they contracted and broke. The pick-up mechanism malfunctioned,

By the mid-1890s, electric traction was dominating transit. Originally powered by steam locomotives, the "L" converted to electric power starting in 1895. Here, a southbound cable train on State Street passes under the Van Buren "L" in 1905, by which time the "L" had developed into a formidable competitor to the cable car. *Chicago History Museum.*

and the slot closed up. When it rained, the conduit flooded; in the winter, it filled with ice and snow. Nevertheless, Yerkes tried for more than two years to make the system work until he finally gave up in 1894.

Yerkes was not the only one promoting this idea. Opposed to overhead wires downtown, the influential and forward-looking Bion Arnold Report of 1902 called the operation of Chicago's transit by electricity "practical and feasible," insisting that the electricity could be provided by wires run through trenches or cable car conduits.

The Transit Titan also experimented with battery power, direct steam and stored steam—anything that would avoid the expense of using horses or building more cable lines. The determined, open-minded Yerkes imported a small steam locomotive (called a dummy) from Belgium that was used on Larrabee Street. Since the city would not allow it to operate downtown, its trailers had to be hauled through the city center by horses. Also, two steam dummies were used on Sheffield Avenue to transport horsecars to Lincoln Avenue cable trains.

In the 1890s, it was more urgent to convert horsecar lines than cable car lines to electric trolley service. Therefore, Chicago's centrally located cable lines became surrounded by networks of trolley lines. This trolley is crossing the Chicago River at Irving Park Road in 1903 when there were still no trolleys downtown. *Chicago Public Library, Northside Neighborhood History Collection.*

Yerkes's most exhaustive experiment involved the Connelly gas motor, an improved version of earlier naphtha gas motors. Powered with standard illuminating gas from city mains, the cars were tested on the Lake and Halsted Streets horsecar lines starting in 1890. Later, NCSR operated them with passengers on the Clark Street, Lincoln Avenue and 5th Avenue (now Wells Street) cable lines as well as on its downtown loop, but most likely only as night cars when the cable did not operate.

The gas motor system showed some promise. The *Street Railway Journal* reported in July 1892 that Yerkes's companies "have concluded to use them extensively on their lines." Yerkes was so hopeful about the technology that he told stockholders that all electrical motors for use on WCSR's outlying roads would be discarded. He even purchased a controlling interest in the Connelly Motor Company and began manufacturing motors.

The noise and "unbearable" smell of the motors, however, generated complaints from the public. Worse, the cars and their fueling devices were prone to explode.

After several explosions, one of which destroyed a car, the City Council banned Connelly motors in November 1893. Yerkes ran the cars anyway and secured an injunction preventing the city from banning them. A car barn fire caused by the gas destroyed thirty-eight cars and ten gas motors, resulting in $75,000 in damages. Finally, in December, the city prevailed in court, and Yerkes gave up on the gas motor.

Yerkes also tested a kinetic motor, "a direct application of the most simple, efficient and reliable form of energy yet discovered or utilized—that of steam," reported the April 1892 *Street Railway Journal*. Rather than boil water to make steam along the way, this car was charged with boiling water every twenty miles or five hours. The hot water kept producing steam thanks to "a simple form of auxiliary heat…completely hidden from view." WCSR used the kinetic motor, but little is known of that test.

Yerkes also experimented with compressed-air cars, operating them on Lake and Halsted Streets starting about 1890. Later, from 1899 to 1906, compressed air cars seating thirty passengers each operated as night cars on Clark Street's cable lines between the Limits car barn and Washington Street, with a stop at the Elm Street powerhouse to recharge their tanks.

ELECTRIC TROLLEY BREAKS THROUGH

Nationwide, the conversion to trolleys was instigated by a successful installation in Montgomery, Alabama, in 1886 by VanDepoele and another in Richmond, Virginia, in 1888 by Frank Sprague. These systems functioned smoothly and cost only a fraction of what it would have cost to build, operate and maintain a comparable cable line.

Streetcar operators from across the country visited the trolley installations to see this marvel for themselves. Most of them were convinced by what they saw and recognized that the tide had turned. After representatives from Boston's West End Street Railway—the nation's largest street railway—inspected Sprague's installation, they made a last-minute decision to convert their horsecar lines to trolley rather than continuing with their previously announced conversion to cable, which had been planned at the urging of Chicago City Railway's President Holmes. Spurred by this influential decision, the change was abrupt. In May 1888, the *Street Railway Journal* stated flatly, "The utility of electricity as a motive-power for propulsion of street-cars is no longer a matter of question."

As electric trolleys proved the most reliable and economical alternative to cable car technology, opposition to dangerous, unsightly overhead wires in city centers dissipated.

Trolleys began to operate downtown after overhead wires were finally allowed there in 1906. Initially, some of the trolleys ran on cable car tracks, as seen in this late 1906 photo of a State Street trolley turning east onto Madison Street, entering a former cable car loop. *Chicago History Museum.*

By 1890, some two hundred companies operated electric railways in the United States, 90 percent of them using Sprague's patents. In 1891, the *Electrical Engineer* editorialized, "Hour by hour, experience is teaching all doubters that the problem of rapid transit for cities has been solved, and that the trolley has come, and come to stay."

The Calumet Electric Street Railway launched Chicago's trolley era, opening the first line on October 2, 1890. It operated two and a half miles principally along 93rd Street from Stony Island to South Chicago Avenues. As other companies built trolley lines, particularly in neighboring towns and outlying areas of Chicago, the once innovative CCR realized that it was falling behind. In 1893, it built three cross-town trolley lines. NCSR followed suit the same year. WCSR (still building cable lines in 1893) did not install its first trolley line until 1895.

Soon, Chicago's street railways sought permission to convert all their lines to trolley for operating uniformity. Permission was granted in dribs and drabs initially for outlying horsecar lines—but still not downtown. Over the next several years, the center of the country's second-biggest city was served by antiquated cable cars during the day and horsecars at night while outlying areas and towns, including Ottawa, Elgin, Rockford and Peoria, Illinois, were served by modern, comfortable electric transit cars. More anomalous was the fact that small, rickety grip cars towed the new larger trolleys downtown.

As late as 1905, CCR ran fourteen million cable car miles and twenty-two million electric trolley car miles. By this time, every flat cable car system in the country had been swept away—except the three in Chicago.

Finally in 1906, by which time trolleys carried 90 percent of Chicago's transit passengers, the Settlement Ordinances granted permission to install trolley wires downtown (as previously discussed). This cleared the way to converting Chicago's cable lines. On the West Side, the last cable cars operated on Madison Street and Milwaukee Avenue on August 19. On the North Side, the last cable cars operated on Lincoln and Clybourn Avenues on October 21. A little later, it was all over when CCR's Cottage Grove Avenue cable line made its last run after almost twenty-five years of operation. This made CCR the nation's longest-running cable car system that addressed general transit needs on a flat terrain.

After 1906, most grip cars were scrapped, but the larger cable trailers were pulled by trolleys in passenger service. For a few years, trolleys ran over the cable tracks, but as they increased in weight (from eight thousand pounds up to twenty-four thousand pounds by the turn of the century), trolleys became too heavy for cable tracks. Most of the cable rails were removed and the tops of the yokes cut off so that new tracks for trolleys could be laid. Removing the entire yokes, underground conduits and vaults, however, was often more trouble than it was worth.

The trolley companies went on to be extremely profitable, primarily due to the efficiency of electric power. Also, it cost only $25,000 to $30,000 to build a mile of trolley line, less than one-quarter the cost of building a cable line.

By 1917, trolleys were carrying more than eleven billion riders a year over nearly forty-five thousand miles of track nationwide. Trolley tracks crisscrossed virtually every city, creating the "streetcar city," an urban design that Donald Miller in *City of the Century* calls "perhaps the most livable of all historical urban forms." By

Until 1906, cable trains towed new trolleys through downtown; afterward, the opposite was true. Trolleys continued to tow old, decrepit cable car trailers for years until enough new trolleys could be purchased.

Old cable cars were put to a variety of uses, including work cars, sheds and offices. This cable car trailer was built in CCR's shop during the run-up to the 1893 World's Columbian Exposition and operated for years on State Street. This photo was published in the *Chicago Daily News* in 1907, and the 1923 Chicago city directory lists the offices of W.M. Crilly at 7922 S. Dorchester Avenue. *Chicago History Museum.*

1933, however, in-street trolleys were gone from half the U.S. cities that once had them. Thereafter, trolleys followed a path similar to that of cable cars—virtually disappearing from the American landscape.

PLAY IT AGAIN...

One cable car staged a last hurrah in Chicago in 1949 during the Chicago Railroad Fair. The Western Pacific Railway sent San Francisco's Powell Street grip car No. 524 to the fair along with three gripmen to operate it. They were chosen for this honor by winning a bell-ringing contest in San Francisco, the first of what became a popular annual event.

What's a cable car doing along Chicago's lakefront? In 1949, San Francisco loaned grip car 524 to the Chicago Railroad Fair. The car provided a popular ride and included an incline as well as a turntable resembling the famous one at the foot of Powell Street in San Francisco. *Jack Doyle and George Kanary collection. Photo by Fred Borchert.*

Carrying capacity loads, the car operated on a slope along Lake Michigan's shore. A working turntable at the top of the incline resembled the famous one at Powell and Market Streets.

CHAPTER 12

CABLE CARS
AROUND THE COUNTRY

S ince Chicago launched a nationwide cable car boom, let's take a look at some of the notable cable car systems found in a surprisingly large number of U.S. cities. All told, sixty-five transit companies built cable lines in twenty-nine cities throughout the country. Many other companies planned to follow suit but did not act before the sun began to set on cable cars in the late 1880s.

Most major U.S. cities of the day, except Atlanta, Boston, Detroit and New Orleans, saw grip cars plying their streets. The installations varied tremendously depending on many factors including terrain, city size, climate, preexisting transit scene and financial conditions. Some lines were successful, technologically and financially. Others were abysmal failures.

Much has already been written about San Francisco's cable cars. Suffice it to say that San Francisco's first cable line in 1873 climbed a steep, 0.5-mile-long hill on Clay Street traveling four miles per hour. By 1890, eight companies had built twenty-three routes crisscrossing the city, culminating in 52.8 double-track miles. In 1906—coincidentally, the same year cable cars ceased operating in Chicago—the San Francisco earthquake and subsequent fire devastated that city's cable car network. Most lines there were rebuilt for trolleys, but three still operate.

The City by the Bay was not the only hilly city to make use of cable cars. Kansas City is so hilly that "one is surprised cable traction was not invented there," said George Hilton in *The Cable Cars of America*. Its cable routes had 5 percent inclines throughout the city and one of the steepest climbs anywhere at 18.5 percent. And hilly Seattle's cable car network was remarkable for two long trestles 140 and 200 feet high.

Denver's lines were distinguished for other reasons. Denver City Cable Railway operated more cables from one powerhouse than any other company. Its two

750-horsepower engines pulled six cables (one of which was seven miles long) that added up to thirty-four miles. Meanwhile, Denver Tramway built the worst-designed cable route. It included twenty turns and curves, twelve at right angles. Due to derailments and excessive cable wear, this line operated for only five weeks. In another fiasco, Denver Tramway beat its competitor to a new route by marshalling 1,600 men to build four blocks of track on Lawrence Street overnight. Nice work, but this track was never used.

Congressional legislation in 1888 requiring that mechanical power take over for horsecars prompted construction of cable lines in Washington, D.C. In 1897, however, a huge fire brought that system to a standstill. Horses were used until cable operations could be resumed, but that never happened, as it became clear that trolleys were a better investment.

Cable cars were not limited to large cities. Butte, Montana, with only 10,723 inhabitants in 1890, had a 1.5-mile line from its center up the side of a nearby mountain. Operated from 1889 to 1897, the line carried primarily workers to their mining jobs.

In Sioux City, Iowa, with only 37,806 inhabitants in 1890, Sioux City Cable Railway was driven by a desire to develop real estate in the hills north of town. Its six-mile cable line was single track, an unusual money-saving configuration that required sidetracks to allow trains to pass each other. Due to plans to build fifty miles of cable lines, little Sioux City had one of the largest powerhouses in the country. Awaiting more cable installations, the plant generated electricity for homes and sold steam to heat buildings. After the land boom went bust, the company declared bankruptcy in 1893.

Cable lines like the one in Sioux City, built to develop real estate, were the least viable and the first to fail. The lines were just too expensive to build, and traffic usually developed slowly on a new line. This became evident starting with Los Angeles's Second Street Cable Railway, which failed in 1889. That same year, Kansas City's Interstate Consolidated Rapid Transit Railway, also conceived of as a means to develop real estate, became the second cable line to fail. This was so early in the history of the trolley that this line was converted to *steam*.

With the distinction of being the coldest city to run cable cars, St. Paul's experience demonstrated that severe winter weather did, indeed, limit the applicability of cable car technology. In a telling sign, a blizzard delayed the opening of St. Paul's first line for several days in 1888. To allow for extreme temperature variations, the slot was made wider than usual, which not only trapped wagon wheels and horseshoe calks but also allowed ice and snow to accumulate in the conduit. Winter was so tough on these lines that some suggested operating the lines only in the summer. Even so, year-round service continued until 1898.

A St. Louis Railroad cable train at Broadway and Pine in 1891. The street is decorated for the Mechanical and Agricultural Fair. *Museum of Transportation.*

The most obscure cable line might have been in Binghamton, New York, where the Washington Street & State Asylum Railroad used cable trackage as part of a steam railway to carry passengers the last mile of its route up a 250-foot-high hill to the state mental hospital. This experimental installation used exposed cables and did not function well. Some semblance of service began in 1885 and lasted only a couple of years.

St. Louis

Like flat Chicago, St. Louis saw one of the largest installations of cable cars with about twenty-eight route miles. Five companies operated cable trains beginning relatively early in 1886.

Built by St. Louis Cable & Western Railway, the first line was operationally challenged, using a single 34,600-foot cable to pull trains over a torturous route including thirteen right-angle curves. Nevertheless, passengers flocked to the line, so much so that two rivals built roughly parallel cable lines, pushing Cable & Western into bankruptcy after three years.

One of the rivals, Missouri Railroad, built a long, straight route between downtown, residential areas and the popular Forest Park. It carried so many passengers and was so profitable that it fueled the misconception widely held nationwide that cable lines were more economical than electric trolley for heavily traveled lines. This led the company to mistakenly re-equip its line with new and better cable cars in 1896, by which time conversion to electric trolleys was already well underway elsewhere.

Even though St. Louis's climate is milder than Chicago's, cold weather presented serious problems to cable car operations there. Slot closures and conduits clogged with ice and snow closed down Citizens' Railway for the entire winter of 1888.

As in Chicago, opposition to overhead wires downtown influenced the decision to stick with cable even after this technology had peaked. St. Louis Railroad, for one, built a cable line as late as 1890. In 1899, St. Louis's major transit companies were consolidated into United Railways, which quickly converted all of the city's cable lines to trolley. More than $6 million was invested in St. Louis's cable car plant; about $3 million of that was a net loss when cable car operations ceased in 1904.

NEW YORK

Given its population density and high transit ridership, New York was an ideal location for cable cars and could have surpassed Chicago in number of riders. Nevertheless, squabbles over patent infringements and the tearing up of streets to install conduits delayed the building of many lines.

The patent trust, which tried to control the cable car technology that had developed in San Francisco, formed the New York Cable Railway in 1883 to "gridiron" the city with an extensive seventy-two-mile system. Despite such grand plans, the company gave up seven years later with nothing to show for its efforts.

Rival Third Avenue Railroad opened a cable line in 1885, as did Metropolitan Street Railway in 1893. Both used non-trust technologies and had limited success, prompting Thomas Edison to predict that New York would "rue the day" it installed cable.

A short cable car turning loop served trains at the south terminus of New York's Third Avenue Railroad cable line, seen here circa 1895. Chicago's cable car turnaround loops, on the other hand, were rectangles running several blocks down the middle of downtown streets. *Courtesy of Stephen Meyers.*

Another disincentive to the development of cable in New York was the decision by both these companies to use a duplicate cable system that required two parallel cables running the same direction in each conduit. This allowed operation to continue even while one of the cables was being repaired or undergoing its daily inspection. And putting both cables in motion and alternating cars between them allowed the lines to handle unusually heavy traffic. But the duplicate cable system was the most capital-intensive design ever, costing almost $1 million per mile overall, several times the industry average. Both companies were quick to electrify their cable lines—Third Avenue in 1899 and Metropolitan in 1901.

BROOKLYN BRIDGE

While Andrew Hallidie, a wire rope manufacturer on the West Coast, was applying his product to pulling railway cars along streets, W.A. Roebling, a wire rope manufacturer on the East Coast, was applying his product to holding up bridges. The two applications came together in 1883 on the Brooklyn Bridge, where several 15¾-inch-diameter cables supported the bridge while 1½-inch-diameter cables pulled cars across the bridge. Instead of running in a conduit, the cable ran in the center of the track, three inches above the rails. Cable cars were used on the bridge rather than steam locomotives to reduce the weight on the bridge and to handle inclines of up to 3.8 percent.

The one-mile bridge was divided into five longitudinal sections. Carriages ran on the two outside sections; cable cars operated on the next two sections; and pedestrians walked along a platform in the center.

This was one of the most unusual—and successful—cable lines in the world. Annual ridership exploded from nine million in 1883 to a remarkable thirty-one million in 1888. Traffic hit twelve thousand riders an hour. "This enormous traffic exceeds the original expectations, and the great, abrupt fluctuations of power required to propel the trains at these busy hours have severely tested the engines," reported *Scientific American*.

New York & Brooklyn Bridge Railway took myriad measures to handle the enormous number of riders, including two- then three- then four-car trains; expanded platforms; shorter headways, down to one and a half minutes between trains; and an improved grip. The most dramatic measure was to build duplicate cable trackage on the same right-of-way in 1893. This involved installing a second cable and a second bank of winding machinery, as well as a second set of rails just inches from the original rails.

Of course, electrification was inevitable. In 1894, electric wires were

The one-mile cable car line on the Brooklyn Bridge might have been the most remarkable cable line in the world. It operated from 1883 until 1908 and carried a huge number of passengers. *New York Public Library.*

strung over the tracks to light the cars. Two years later, the company introduced electrically powered cars to switch cable cars at crossovers at either end of the line. Still, it did not discontinue cable car operations until 1908.

SAN DIEGO

When San Diego Cable Railway began to operate its 4.7-mile cable line in 1890, the town had only 16,159 inhabitants. Similar to many other ill-fated cable lines, this line was designed to develop real estate, connecting suburban steam railroad depots with developing residential areas north of town. An unusual single-track, two-way operation meant that two cables ran through the conduit, requiring the gripman to select either the uphill or the downhill cable. Trains going in opposite directions passed each other on sidetracks.

Demonstrating the fluidity between competing transit technologies in the 1880s and 1890s, San Diego Cable Railway was one of a handful of companies that installed its cable line *after* an earlier *electric* line had failed.

As many street railways did before and since, the company created an attraction at the end of its line to encourage people to ride its trains. Overlooking the Mission Valley, this small park called The Bluffs blossomed into Mission Cliff Gardens, one of the country's most beautiful botanical gardens.

The line was one of the country's least successful and shortest-lived cable operations. It was shut down after just two years and four months due to the failure of the bank that had financed the company. Accidents, a sagging economy, the lack of real estate development in the targeted residential areas and the construction of a rival electric line did not help, either.

ෂෑ

The complete list of U.S. cities with cable car transit lines in order of their first installation follows. It contains some surprises. Is your city on the list? New York City; San Francisco; Chicago; Philadelphia; Kansas City, Missouri; Cincinnati; Los Angeles; Binghamton, New York; Hoboken, New Jersey; St. Louis; Oakland, California; Brooklyn, New York; Omaha, Nebraska; St. Paul, Minnesota; Newark, New Jersey; Grand Rapids, Michigan; Pittsburgh; Seattle; Denver; Butte, Montana; Sioux City, Iowa; Spokane, Washington; Providence, Rhode Island; Portland, Oregon; Washington, D.C.; San Diego; Cleveland; Baltimore; and Tacoma, Washington. In addition, major lines were proposed but never built in Dallas; St.

Joseph, Missouri; Boston; Minneapolis; Milwaukee; and Lincoln, Nebraska.

The last city to see an initial cable car installation was Tacoma, where in 1890, the main business district was located at water level while the secondary business district and residential areas were located up a steep hill. The Tacoma Railway & Motor Company used a 1.8-mile, single-track rectangular cable car loop to negotiate the hill, connecting electric trolley lines that it was building at the same time.

Hilly Tacoma, hilly Seattle and hilly San Francisco were the last three U.S. cities to operate cable cars. The technology found itself back where it started: an expensive, novel yet effective way to climb steep hills. Tacoma discontinued its line in 1938, and Seattle discontinued its last lines in 1940. That left only San Francisco. Today, the cable car is primarily a tourist attraction, although many locals depend on it for transportation.

CHAPTER 13

CHICAGO'S CABLE CAR REMNANTS

The remnants of Chicago's cable car story are plentiful—if you know where to look. The vestiges vary from buildings to the lack of buildings; from track structures hidden underground to cable cars on display at museums; from a simple wisp of a cable car ticket for sale on eBay to an impressive observatory equipped with the largest refracting telescope in the world.

Jonathan Michael Johnson's color photographs—commissioned for this book—show the interiors and exteriors of some of the still-standing structures. These exquisite photographs pay homage to Chicago's cable car era and breathe new life into old bricks and mortar.

The most prominent remnants of Chicago's cable car story are two powerhouses, massive and impressive in their day but weathered and worn today. The crown jewel is the North Chicago Street Railroad's former powerhouse at LaSalle and Illinois Streets. This three-story structure was built at an estimated cost of $35,000 in 1888. "It was a striking presence in the River North area, which was a jumble of low-scale factories, warehouses and shipyards," says a Commission on Chicago Landmarks Designation Report from 2000.

In 2001, the building was designated a Chicago Landmark, which stipulates that any work to it is reviewed to ensure that historical and architectural features are preserved. Alas, this was not always the case, as the structure has been significantly modified. In 1910, a forty-five- by fifty-foot portion at the building's rear northwest corner was removed to make room for the construction of an electrical substation for trolleys. The substation remains an electrical facility of the Chicago Transit Authority. The powerhouse's original smokestack, which was more than seventy-five feet tall, was probably removed at the same time.

The former cable car powerhouse at LaSalle and Illinois Streets has served many purposes, most famously as Michael Jordan's Restaurant. It is now the LaSalle Power Co., a multilevel entertainment venue, with a stage and dance hall on the top floor. *Photo by Jonathan Michael Johnson.*

More significant, the building's LaSalle Street façade was moved seventeen feet west of its original location when the street was widened in 1929. Although this modification reduced the size of the building, workers faithfully re-created the front exterior so the building is largely intact. "It has good integrity, retaining those exterior physical features most closely associated with its historic appearance and that convey its historic visual character…including important masonry details," according to the report. The two street façades are faced with finely textured red pressed brick, while the side and back are built of common brick.

Since the cable car steam engines were shut down in 1906, the building has been abandoned, was later used as an automobile repair shop and subsequently housed two restaurants: Ireland's and Michael Jordan's. The latter displayed a huge basketball on the roof of the building. Currently, the building houses LaSalle Power Co., a multilevel entertainment venue.

Much less famed is the West Chicago Street Railroad's former powerhouse still standing at Washington and Jefferson Streets. For decades, this building housed the Chicago Surface Lines' Legal and Accident Investigation Department. Subsequently, it was modified more substantially—perhaps unalterably—than the other powerhouse. Several dormers were added at the roofline, the rear portion of the building was extended and the smokestack was removed. Worse, a garish stone façade covers the ground floor. Today, the building serves as headquarters for Local 134 of the International Brotherhood of Electrical Workers, which hosts the monthly meeting of the 20th Century Railroad Club.

Other former cable car powerhouse sites are conspicuous by the absence of a contemporary building there. A Chicago City Railway powerhouse was located at the northeast corner of Cottage Grove Avenue and 55th Street where today there is a large, grassy open space in front of the Friend Family Health Center.

This former WCSR powerhouse at Jefferson and Washington Streets drove the cables that pulled West Side cable cars through the tunnel under the South Branch of the Chicago River and around two downtown loops. Drastically modified, the building is now the International Brotherhood of Electrical Workers' Local 134 headquarters. *Photo by Jonathan Michael Johnson.*

A WCSR powerhouse was located at the northeast corner of Jefferson and Van Buren Streets where today there is only a parking lot. And a NCSR powerhouse was located on Sheffield Avenue between Wrightwood and Lill Avenues where Jonquil Park sits today. These former powerhouse sites lack buildings because the massive underground cable car infrastructure (including foundations, vaults and equipment) that was left behind would have to be removed before substantial buildings could be constructed there. In many cases, it is not worth the expense to remove such huge, heavy ruins. For example, the concrete foundation for the machinery in the sixty- by one-hundred-foot engine room of CCR's powerhouse on Cottage Grove Avenue was twenty-three feet deep.

Cable car infrastructure also lies hidden underneath many Chicago streets. Neither the cable car companies nor the City of Chicago ever made a systematic effort to remove the conduits and accompanying vaults. Instead, the cable car tracks and the tops of the yokes were removed to allow electric trolley tracks to be built. Occasionally,

Right: The exterior of the former WCSR cable car storage barn at 2524 S. Blue Island Avenue, built in 1892. This photo shows the rear of the building at Coulter Street and Bell Avenue. *Photo by Jonathan Michael Johnson.*

Below: The interior of the former WCSR cable car storage barn at 2524 S. Blue Island Avenue. The building houses Sorini Ring Manufacturing, which claims to be the longest-running family-owned business in the drum ring industry. *Photo by Jonathan Michael Johnson.*

street repair projects unearth remaining cable car remnants, causing unforeseen delays and additional expenses.

Car barns were less massive than powerhouses. A former WCSR cable car storage barn built in 1892 still stands at 2524 S. Blue Island Avenue. Today, Sorini Ring Manufacturing uses it as a factory to make rings for oil drums and storage containers. Comparing the current building with old photographs shows that the second floor of this structure was removed or the façade shortened.

Two buildings on Armitage Avenue west of Campbell Avenue were part of a large complex of as many as eight structures at the end of WCSR's Milwaukee Avenue cable line. This complex included cable car and horsecar barns, a stable, a blacksmith shop and a carwash, some of which dated back to 1878. Only two of these structures remain. One is a food warehouse, and the other appears to be used for manufacturing and as a studio.

A still smaller cable car building remains at 5529 S. Lake Park Avenue along what was once the cable car loop at the end of CCR's 55th Street cable line. CCR built it

Built in 1885, this building on Armitage Avenue at Stave Street was part of a large complex at the end of WCSR's Milwaukee Avenue cable line. *Photo by Jonathan Michael Johnson.*

The interior of a former WCSR building on Armitage Avenue west of Campbell Avenue. The current owner reports that the chain and ring to the left of the door remain from cable car days. *Photo by Jonathan Michael Johnson.*

in 1893 in anticipation of the heavy traffic that the World's Columbian Exposition would generate. This makes it one of the few structures remaining that has a tie to the fair.

The building's original purpose remains unknown, but CCR probably built it as a waiting room for trainmen—a place for them to eat, congregate, wait between runs and use the restroom. Part of the building could have been open to cable car passengers and/or used to sell tickets.

It is surprising that this small building still survives. As early as 1898, it was converted to a lunchroom, which it remained for decades under different owners. The best-known restaurant located there was Steve's Lunch, which was open from about 1948 to 1966. Dilapidated by 1977, the building was used to store pushcarts for a newspaper delivery service. The building was beautifully but not necessarily accurately refurbished in 1981. Today, it is the home of the Hyde Park Historical Society; as such, it is frequently open for public viewing and/or programs.

The underground entrance to Carroll Street in the center of LaSalle Street at Kinzie Street seems like it should be a cable car vestige—but it is not. There was a cable car tunnel under the river at approximately the same location, but it was deeper than the current underground passageway and surfaced a block north at Michigan (now Hubbard) Street. NCSR cable cars ran through the original tunnel to and from downtown, pulled by a cable issued from the powerhouse at Illinois and LaSalle Streets. The original tunnel was used during the construction of the Milwaukee-Dearborn Subway (now the Blue Line) and then filled in 1953.

There are only two Chicago cable cars to visit, both built by the Chicago Surface Lines in the 1930s. Although only replicas, they are accurate and realistic. The original CCR grip car 532 plied State Street, whereas the replica traveled around the city, including in parades and for a stint at a major downtown department store. Since 1938, it has been on display at the Museum of Science and Industry, where visitors can sit on the car and look in a trench underneath the car to see how its grip once worked. CCR 209, the other replica, is on display at the Illinois Railway Museum in Union, Illinois, about sixty miles west of Chicago. It is depicted on the back cover of this book. Available for viewing only, this closed trailer seated thirty passengers.

Farther away, you can visit the Yerkes Observatory, about ninety miles northwest of Chicago on the shore of Lake Geneva in Williams Bay, Wisconsin. Chicago Cable Car Czar Charles Tyson Yerkes funded this 1897 building and its huge forty-inch refracting telescope to burnish his public image.

Above: This portal at LaSalle and Kinzie Streets serves Carroll Avenue and nearby loading docks. The portal that NCSR cable cars entered to cross under the Chicago River from 1888 to 1906 was one block north at Austin Avenue (now Hubbard Street). The original portal was filled in and paved over in 1953. *Photo by Jonathan Michael Johnson.*

Opposite: CCR's former cable car "waiting room" now sits alongside Metra's commuter tracks at 5529 S. Lake Park Avenue. Since 1977, it has served as the Hyde Park Historical Society's headquarters. The interior has been significantly modified. *Photo by Jonathan Michael Johnson.*

Finally, the Cable Car Museum in San Francisco is highly recommended. The two-story 1887 building houses San Francisco Municipal Railway's car barn and working powerhouse that drives all four cables used by the city's remaining three cable lines. Visitors' galleries provide clear views of how the cables circulate underground and through the winding machinery.

Riding San Francisco's cable cars, designated a National Historic Landmark in 1964, is the best way to get a feel for what Chicago's cable cars were like. It is very telling that the cable car technology is still about the same, even though Chicago's cable cars stopped operating in 1906. The major difference between a cable car ride in Chicago in 1882 and one in San Francisco 130 years later is the City by the Bay's hills.

AFTERWORD

Almost ten years ago, before I wrote my first book about Chicago, an established author advised me to write about something other than Chicago history. The field was already covered, even saturated, he said. It seemed as though he was correct. So many local topics and figures had already been written about, and the Chicago sections of local bookstores were full to bursting.

Since then, more than two hundred new books have been published about Chicago history. Some of my favorites are *The Merchant of Power* by John Wasik, *Sin in the Second City* by Karen Abbott and *Giants in the Park* by Krista August. The plethora of new titles shows that there have been and probably still are many stones still unturned and a never-ending number of stories to tell about our incredible city. Indeed, some local authors and publishers keep coming up with more—and more interesting—titles. The prolific author Richard Lindberg recently added *The Gambler King of Clark Street* to his impressive list of books. The inexhaustible Sharon Woodhouse, founder of Lake Claremont Press, continues to publish a parade of vital local titles, such as the recent *Carless in Chicago* by Jason Rothstein. And masters of their art Richard Cahan and Michael Williams have added yet another gem, *The Lost Panoramas*, to their magnificent oeuvre.

I hope that *Chicago's Cable Cars* will add to this momentum. Who knows how many other subjects are out there, waiting to be discovered, explored or reevaluated?

I also hope this book will inspire people—students, writers, book clubs, the public, professionals, politicians—to study Chicago's history more thoroughly. There are holes in our knowledge of local history, as demonstrated by the incredible fact that our cable car story was virtually forgotten, even though during twenty-five years—a period of time that included the ever-popular World's Columbian Exposition—

CCR cable car 532 on display in a downtown department store before it was moved to the Museum of Science and Industry, where it has been on display since 1938. Little or nothing on the car is original, but the car is an accurate replica. *Chicago Transit Authority.*

Chicago's cable cars carried more than one *billion* riders, everyone from the likes of Daniel Burnham, Chicago's great urban planner, to Henry Howard Holmes, Chicago's notorious serial killer.

Finally, I hope this book will lead to some kind of recognition for Chicago's cable cars: a plaque, a monument, some new signage, a seminar, a festival, or even the construction of a short cable car line, perhaps on Navy Pier running past the Ferris wheel, the original version of which coincided in more than one way with Chicago's cable cars. A statue of Chicago Cable Car Czar Charles Tyson Yerkes or an honorary street named after him would be extremely appropriate and is long overdue.

In the meantime, I'd settle for a worn piece of cable or a rusty pulley unearthed by the next street renovation project.

BIBLIOGRAPHY

Books, Typescripts and Theses

Asbury, Herbert. *Gangs of Chicago: An Informal History of Chicago*. New York: Alfred A. Knopf, 1940.

Buckley, James J. "Chicago City Railway Company." Unpublished typescript.

Buckley, James J., and Roy G. Benedict. "Chicago's West Division Street Railways in the 1800s." Unpublished typescript.

Buckley, R.J. *A History of Tramways, from Horse to Rapid Transit*. North Pomfret, VT: David & Charles, 1975.

Carson, Robert. *Whatever Happened to the Trolley?* Washington, D.C.: University Press of America, 1978.

Cudahy, Brian. *Cash, Tokens and Transfers: A History of Urban Mass Transit in North America*. New York: Fordham University Press. 1990.

———. *A Century of Service*. Washington, D.C.: American Public Transit Association, 1982.

Duis, Perry. *Challenging Chicago: Coping with Everyday Life, 1837–1920*. Urbana: University of Illinois Press, 1998.

Duke, Thomas. *Celebrated Criminal Cases of America*. San Francisco: James Barry Company, 1910.

Fairchild, Charles. *Street Railways: Their Construction, Operation and Maintenance*. New York: Street Railway Publishing Company, 1892.

Fischler, Stanley. *Moving Millions*. New York: Harper & Row, 1979.

Franch, Robert. *Robber Baron*. Urbana: University of Illinois Press, 2006.

Hanscom, W. *The Archaeology of the Cable Car*. Pasadena, CA: Socio-Technical Books, 1970.

Harter, Jim. *World Railways of the Nineteenth Century*. Baltimore, MD: Johns Hopkins University Press, 2005.

Hilton, George. *The Cable Car in America*. Berkeley, CA: Howell-North Books, 1971.

Holtzer, Susan. *Cable Car Confidential*. San Francisco: Caddo Gap Press, 2002.

Inter Ocean staff. *A History of the City of Chicago: Its Men and Institutions*. Chicago: *Inter Ocean*, 1900.

Johnson, James. *A Century of Chicago Streetcars, 1858–1958*. Wheaton, IL: Traction Orange Company, 1964.

Long, Bryant Alden. *Mail by Rail*. New York: Simmons-Boardman, 1951.

Mason, John, and Raymond Flemming. *Street Car R.P.O. Service in Chicago*. Chicago: Mobile Post Office Society, 1983.

Middleton, William. *Time of the Trolley*. San Marino, CA: Golden West Books, 1987.

Miller, Donald. *City of the Century*. New York: Simon & Schuster, 1996.

Miller, John Anderson. *Fares Please!* New York: Dover Publications, 1941.

Moses, John, and Joseph Kirkland. *Aboriginal to Metropolitan: History of Chicago*. Chicago: Munsell & Co., 1895.

Nordahl, Darrin. *My Kind of Transit: Rethinking Public Transportation in America*. Chicago: Center for American Places at Columbia College, 2008.

Norton, Samuel Wilber. *Chicago Traction: A History Legislative and Political*. Chicago: Samuel Wilber Norton, 1907.

Pierce, Bessie Louise. *A History of Chicago, Volume III: The Rise of a Modern City, 1871–1893*. New York: Alfred A. Knopf, 1957.

Pushkarev, Boris. *Urban Rail in America*. Bloomington: Indiana University Press, 1892.

Sandler, Martin. *Straphanging in the USA*. Oxford, UK: Oxford University Press, 2003.

Smallwood, Charles, Warren Edward Miller and Don DeNevi. *The Cable Car Book*. New York: Bonanza Books, 1980.

Smith, J. Bucknall, and George Hilton. *A Treatise Upon Cable or Rope Traction*. Philadelphia: Owlswick Press, 1977.

Stead, William. *If Christ Came to Chicago*. Chicago: Laird & Lee, 1894.

Swan, Christopher. *Cable Car*. Berkeley, CA: Ten Speed Press, 1973.

Taylor, Troy. *Murder and Mayhem on Chicago's South Side*. Charleston, SC: The History Press, 2009.

Weber, Robert David. "Rationalizers and Reformers." Doctoral thesis, University of Wisconsin, 1971.

White, John, Jr. *Horsecars, Cable Cars and Omnibuses*. New York: Dover Publications, 1974.

Wright, Augustine. *American Street Railways: Their Construction, Equipment and Maintenance*. New York: Rand, McNally & Company, 1888.

Young, David. *Chicago Transit*. DeKalb: Northern Illinois University Press, 1998.

REPORTS, BULLETINS, PAMPHLETS AND GUIDES

Bard, Edmund. "The Street Railways of Chicago: Report of the Civic Federation of Chicago." Chicago: Municipal Affairs, 1901.

Black, James. *The Street Railroad Situation in Chicago.* Chicago: James S. Black, 1898.

City Council of Chicago. "Report of Special Committee of the City Council of Chicago on the Street Railway Franchises and Operations." Chicago: John F. Higgins, 1898.

Commission on Chicago Landmarks. *LaSalle Street Cable Car Powerhouse.* Chicago: Department of Planning and Development, 2000.

Hilton, George. "Cable Railways of Chicago: Bulletin No. 10." Chicago: Electric Railway Historical Society, 1954.

North Chicago Street Railroad. *The North Chicago Street Railroad and Its Lines.* Chicago: North Chicago Street Railroad, 1889.

Rand, McNally & Company's Bird's-eye Views and Guide to Chicago. Chicago: Rand, McNally & Company, 1893.

"Report of the General Superintendent of Police of the City of Chicago to the City Council." City of Chicago, 1903.

"Report of the Postmaster-General of the United States." Washington, D.C.: Government Printing Office, 1895.

Windsor, H.H. *A Short Description of the Cable System as Operated by the Chicago City Railway.* Chicago: Chicago City Railway, 1887.

Yerkes, Charles Tyson, Hiram Crawford and Fred Threedy. *The Cable Line Illustrated.* Chicago: North Chicago Street Railroad, circa 1888.

WEBSITES

White, John H., Jr. *Horsecars: City Transit Before the Age of Electricity.* www.spec.lib.muohio. edu/Horse%20Car%20brochure-for-website.pdf.

www.cable-car-guy.com.

www.encyclopedia.chicagohistory.org.

www.postalmuseum.si.edu/exhibits/2b1c4_streetcar.html.

BIBLIOGRAPHY

NEWSPAPERS

Chicago Daily News
Chicago Evening Journal
Chicago Times
Chicago Tribune
Hyde Park Herald
Inter Ocean
Morning Courier & New-York Enquirer
New York Herald
New York Times

MAGAZINES

American Geographic Society's Focus on Geography
Chicago History
CTA Transit News
Electrical Engineer
Journal of the Illinois State Historical Society
Railway Age
Route 66 Magazine
Science
Scientific American
Smithsonian
Street Railway Journal
Street Railway Review

ABOUT THE AUTHOR

Born on the Northwest Side of Chicago, Borzo has spent most of his life in Chicago. He is active in many of the city's cultural, historical, bicycling and writing circles.

Borzo has a bachelor's degree in cultural anthropology from Grinnell College and a master's degree in journalism from Northwestern University. In addition to having completed hundreds of freelance articles, he has been a full-time reporter, editor and/or writer at *Modern Railroads Magazine*, *Traffic World*, International Thompson Transport Press, The Business Word, American Medical Association, Field Museum, *Momentum Magazine* and University of Chicago.

Borzo is the author of three other books about Chicago: *The Windies' City* (Highlights of Chicago Press, 2006), a trove of some of Chicago's hidden historical treasures; *The Chicago "L"* (Arcadia Publishing, 2007), a history of Chicago's greatest working antique and biggest "mover and shaker"; and *Where to Bike Chicago: Best Biking in City and Suburbs* (BA Press, 2011), which describes, rates, photographs and maps the seventy-two best bike rides around Chicagoland.

His next book will be *RAGBRAI: America's Favorite Bike Ride* (The History Press, 2013). This book will cover the history and experience of the forty-year-old Register's Annual Great Bike Ride Across Iowa, which attracts tens of thousands of cyclists every year.

Borzo has won several awards, most notably an Alumni Award from Grinnell College and two Peter Lisagor Awards, the leading measure of top-quality journalism in the Chicago area.

Greg currently works as an independent writer. He is an accomplished public speaker and conducts tours about bicycles, the "L" and cable cars for the Chicago History Museum, the Chicago Cycling Club and others—by bike, on the "L" and on foot.

Greg lives in the South Loop (across from the magnificent Harold Washington Library Center) to better enjoy all the culture and history; art and architecture; music and theater; and walking, biking and "L" opportunities that Chicago has to offer. He can be reached at gborzo@comcast.net.